Praise for A Man's Guide -
Navigating the mystery of the menstrual mood swing

Finally, I have a way to read the signs from my flat mate and women I work with. I think is is going to help me in my future relationships too.
Melvin Bertagna

I'm finding that I relate better with my teenage daughter and am walking alongside her rather than against her in a state of confusion.
Derek J

Now when my partner goes from hot to cool I know that she's not rejecting me - that it's just a change in pace and I can meet her there. It takes us even deeper and I love it!
Mark Gavins

Disclaimer

All the information, techniques, skills and concepts contained within this publication are of the nature of general comment only and are not in any way recommended as individual advice. The intent is to offer a variety of information to provide a wider range of options now and going forward, recognising that we are widely diverse in our personal circumstances and opinions and beliefs. Should any reader choose to make use of the information here, this is their individual decision, and the contributors (and their companies) and the author do not assume any responsibilities whatsoever under any condition or circumstances. It is recommended that the reader obtain their own independent advice.

First Edition 2019

Copyright 2019 Meghan Forrester
ISBN 978-0-6487157-1-9

All rights reserved. No part of this work may be reproduced by any means, electronic or mechanical, including photocopying and recording, or by any information storage or retrieval system, except as may be expressly permitted in writing from the publisher.

Dedicated to Tanya Ormsby 1971-2019
Wise Woman ~ Maiden ~ Mother ~ Medicine Woman

Contents

Foreward 6
Preface 9
Acknowledgements 12
The Evohe Story 13
In A Nutshell 17
Not Only Is There A Man's Guide, We Have One For Women Too 18
Introduction 20
How To Get The Most Out Of This Book 23
28 Day Women's Menstrual Cycle 25
Let's Look At Your Why 26
My Why 27
The Science (Short Version) 29
If She Were A Car... The 4 Stages 30
Cycles, Seasons & Archetypes 31
The Dark Side 33
The Good News 36
Risk/Benefit Ratio 37
Let's Get Back To The Simple Solution 39
Winter 40
    Tools For Her In Winter And How You Can Support 41
    When It Comes To Touch 45
Spring 47
    Tools For Her In Spring And How You Can Support 48
    When It Comes To Touch 53
Summer 54
    Tools For Her In Summer And How You Can Support 55
    When It Comes To Touch 59

Autumn 60
   Powerful Medicine Time (PMT) 61
   Tools For Her In Autumn And How You Can Support 62
   When It Comes To Touch 67
Quick Guide For What To Do In Each Season 68
Embodiment 69
The Yin & Yang Of It All 71
The Inner Marriage 72
Yin Qualities 72
Underdeveloped Yin 72
Overdeveloped Yin 72
Yang Qualities 72
Underdeveloped Yang 72
Overdeveloped Yang 72
The Inner Marriage 73
A Question We Hear Often From Men 74
How To Speak Your Partner's Love Language 75
Men Have Cycles Too! 76
Mens Resource Page 77
Men Who've Got Your Back 77
In Summary 78
Resources & References 80
Practitioners 84
About Meg 96
Appendix And Contributing Articles 97

Suppose you cut a tall bamboo in two
Make the bottom piece a woman,
The headpiece a man;
Rub them together till they kindle:
Tell me now,
The fire that's born,
Is it male or female?

Devara Dasimaya,
Tenth Century Shaivite Poet

Foreward

Meghan has written the guide many of us men should have read years ago, had it been available. Far more than just to gain a better understanding of female biology, but to give us the knowledge of how to truly show up in our relationships with women. This deep wisdom allows us to add masculine depth to their cyclical nature and create a whole far more powerful than the sum of the parts. We're in this together, and when a woman feels this energetically, the raging fire of love burns brightest.

I was introduced to Meghan by a girlfriend in 2009. Back then, I was at a crossroads in my life. My younger sister's recent death had rocked me, my mother was gravely ill, and I found myself on a rickety bridge between a corporate world that had disillusioned me and something else I didn't quite understand. I yearned to explore this pull forwards into the unknown and Meghan seemed to somehow represent where I was going. I was drawn to her energy and over the next decade we stayed in close contact as life continued to unfold. A year later, my mother died and I was diagnosed with blood cancer. Five years on, Meghan lost her partner Barry to the same disease. However, in the space between, I transitioned into a meditation teacher and men's coach, while Meghan – among other feats too numerous to mention – continued to build her skincare brand EVOHE. Perhaps most miraculously, we now each have young sons of a similar age.

In the midst of this chaos, Meghan has delivered a thoughtful and illuminating guide for men. You see, most of us fall well short of the pass mark when it comes to understanding true feminine nature. Consider the stereotypical perception of a woman's attitude at 'that' time of the month – what's even less understood is how our own behaviour is influenced by the very same cycle. This forms part of the cosmic dance in which we men must fully engage.

On a different note, from a scientific viewpoint, there's multiple studies to suggest that men consistently rate women who are ovulating as more attractive – we even make riskier decisions during this time of their cycle. Some of this research was based on simply smelling a woman's t-shirt, without her even in it! Our internal chemistry is sending us messages that we are, for the most part, ignoring or consciously unaware of.

These are just small, but tangible examples of how this guide can help break down these age-old narratives, allowing deep healing on both an individual level for men and women – and for our relationships at large.

In this way, we can also support the process of healing and rejuvenation for our intimate partner. We need to remember that our cock is medicine. However, just like any medicine, if used in the wrong way or at the inappropriate time, it can quickly become poison. Much of this comes down to intention and understanding.

We are so often going against our biological programming and not listening to the subtleties, which is where our true nature resides. We need to look beneath the surface if we want to reclaim our sovereignty and tap into a depth of union that may have been previously unimaginable. Not to suggest for a moment that this journey will be easy, but this guide can act as a compass, helping you stay the course.

There is an intense love that goes into everything Meghan does, from a simple conversation, to building EVOHE, to these pages. To read them is a felt experience of her ethos, her values, her mission as a human being. It is an expression of her own life, one which, as a dear friend, I am honoured to share the path.

With love.

Ash

Asher Packman
President, Meditation Australia
Founder, The Fifth Direction

Preface

Dear Men,

in the pages to follow I will offer many suggestions of ways that you can give to the women in your life, some of these ways you may already know, some will be new and some will just sound like I'm speaking another language. I do not ask that you give without first receiving yourself. Please hear me on this.

Giving without receiving is what can often leave a bitter taste in our mouths and so I invite you to experience for yourself the very suggestions that I make in this book. Try some of it on for yourself. See it as a dress rehearsal, a practice run. So that when you do feel to make some of these offerings to the women in your life, you will know yourself how it feels, you may even enjoy it!

With the acknowledgement that her needs and your needs matter equally, we can each let go of any underlying resentment and truly show up as the best versions of ourselves.

Within your very Masculine body or "Yang-ness" is just the right amount of Feminine or "Yin-ness". Both men and women have both of the parts within, and when we care for both, we nourish the whole. It has the effect of smoothing out rough edges, taking the pressure off and calming our nervous systems. This then gives you the ability to find balance and with a sense of maturity and fullness, you can be in an overflow, enabling a sense of loving presence to be the foundation of your life with the women in your life.

When a woman is in her time of bleeding, her natural state is to receive and not give back. As such, similarly, you wouldn't ask a woman in labour to take out the rubbish or make dinner. Her cyclic nature dictates, a woman's bleeding time is the time for her to hold back from giving so that she can replenish, blossom and be ready to share her fruits in the coming weeks. If she is in a state of chronic tiredness there can be some delay here as recovery is a process that requires space and time.

Thank you for your presence and willingness to read this.
How the book came about: I had had many a conversation about my menstrual cycle and sexuality over cups of tea with girlfriends.

What I hadn't done much of was to have this conversation with men. So I asked one, "would you like to have a weekly phone call with me where we discuss the part of my cycle I am in and how it relates sexually?"

His short answer was, "f*** yeah!!!"

Enter, James Brown.

James would turn up for these conversations eager, without distractions and ready to listen. He was a willing participant, he held a safe space and added copious amounts of humour which made it so much easier for me. He also asked courageous questions and called me out when I was holding back.

In a way this book is like you being a fly on the wall for some of those conversations.

I happened to mention this interaction I was having with James to another dear male friend of mine who was quick to say, I want to hear more!

Enter, Asher Packman.

Not only did Asher want to hear more, but he also wanted me to come and share my experience with his men's group! WTF!!!?? Not what I expected.

My short answer, "no way, it's too personal!".

Thanks to a deep trust I have for Asher and his wise insistence and encouragement I ended up agreeing to it and felt surprisingly inspired and excited.

Then the dread crept in and I felt like I was going to throw up from fear. What had I agreed to!?

To calm my nerves a little, I thought I could do some preparation, write notes, make a handout, a visual aid…anything!.

I sat down and started to type. I didn't realise I had so much to say about the topic. I felt like I was speaking to men to ease their discomfort and confusion, I felt like I was speaking for women to ease their anguish and pain. I felt a common humanity, a love for you reading and a love for myself as I healed my own wounds in the pages before me.

A couple of days later I had most of the content you will see from here on in.

I really hope it helps.

Acknowledgements

I exhale with a smile.

I feel love and appreciation for the support I have been given to be able to bring 'it all' together.

Oceans of gratitude to all my beautiful 'test subjects' who shared so openly with me their experiences so that I might give context and clarity to the views I put across in this book.

To the mentors I learn from and appreciate - by playing in your fields, I have learnt in my own style and language and you have so graciously allowed me to do this.

Big respect and future adventures!

A deep gratitude to the men and women who have added their thread to the tapestry - in the form of the Appendix at the end of this book. Moira Williams, Jo Brown, Sharon Maloney, Deborah Oberon and Filippa Araki. You are such powerful elders in my community and you enrichen us all.

To Angela Fitzgerald Marion, and Trace Steph who walked with me in the downpour as I retold my birth story and emerged from the ashes. To my sister who has journeyed with me from my very first day and who holds such a mighty love to keep our family intact and to the women in my inner circle who help me re parent and be my best friend. Caron, Kim, Lissa and Filippa I wouldn't be the woman I am today or the mother I am today without your unwavering support. I love you without my makeup on.

And to the brave men who I call my friends. Scott, James, Asher, Vincent, Kristian, Peter, Mark, Brett, Steve, Kyle, Juan, Satoshi, Loki, Murray, Tez, Marty, Jamo, Footy Shorts, Tom, Lee. I trust you. Thank you for seeing me and loving me as I am.

The EVOHE Story

Now there's a story.

Let me first tell you how we came across this word.

My late husband and I were running an illegal restaurant in the hills of the Byron shire in Australia. We were a thriving combination of man meets woman = lets create something!!!

We had both come from fairly traumatic experiences and were keen to start anew. What we lacked was any real business sense or funding, hence the home-based business. Our clientele loved what we produced and we were booked out for a year, but we also knew that in reality it was a short term gig. Partly because it was illegal and partly because after hand making everything we served, there wasn't really any profit. It was a love job.

One of our very dear customers also pointed this out and asked what our plans were for the future.

It was a poignant moment. I didn't have an answer. But Baz did.

He said, "Meg is going to start a skincare company."
I said, "Hell no, that's not my thing anymore!"

You see, I had been involved with the high end French cosmetic houses in my 20s and I had completely burnt out from the pressure.

The pressure to be manicured, have perfect hair, and walk in heels and not have lipstick on my teeth.

Fun at first but agony by the end of it. There was no way I wanted any part of an industry that used 14 year old models to sell a cellulite cream, or an industry that constantly told me I wasn't pretty enough.

At my defensive response our customer Margie (who we like to call the fairy godmother of EVOHE) and Baz both reassured me that I could do it differently.

It was their belief in me that started this whole EVOHE journey. And since both of them have now passed it is EVOHE that continues to hold me up when my belief in myself falters. What a gift, what a legacy they left to me.

Just with the simple process of applying my moisturiser in the evening and looking myself in the eye with love, I feel held.

And there were many times where it did more than just hold me. The values that EVOHE represent have been a life line to my sanity and a catalyst to my creativity. EVOHE to this day helps me to shed old beliefs and conditioning around not being enough. It has shown me how to turn up with authenticity and belonging in myself, that I can be the real me and that I am totally loveable as I am. Who would have thought that running a business like EVOHE for 12 years would be one of the most transformational tools for personal development and self-awareness.

Baz was a mad keen sailor and he first found the word EVOHE on the side of a boat that regularly sails in the Antarctic. It was our dream to go on expedition with them some day.

Upon further research Baz discovered that the word EVOHE was used by the ancient Greeks and Egyptians when they were dancing and celebrating- as a point of exclamation. So the word EVOHE is basically an exclamation mark! Pretty cool!

After both having come through intense hardships in our life we were determined to Celebrate Life and so the name EVOHE was a fit.

Upon deeper contemplation we realised that when the word was separated into its parts it was EV (woman) O (earth) HE (man).

Our representation of this and what we wove into the very foundations of our business EVOHE is - Celebration of Life and Balance between Man Woman and Earth.

We also used a combination of Australian Bush Flower essences which for me represented the essence of how I wanted to see the Cosmetic industry change. This blend of flowers essentially means, "I see the beauty in myself and I see the beauty in others." How I wish that was what the Beauty Industry was founded on today. My voice still feels small in this industry of giants constantly pumping out messages of "you aren't beautiful as you are".

Our tagline is, 'EVOHE lets you be the real you' and this message is heard by a passionate loyal number of customers who love EVOHE and wouldn't use anything else.

Apart from it being totally natural and palm oil free, our ethical foundations are what I believe have given EVOHE longevity in a not so ethical industry.

Although I've shed many tears and rage at the challenges I've faced running a business in this broken system, I'm also super proud and wouldn't change a moment of it! I can't believe I'm saying this now since I've been so pissed off about it for such a long time, but I am. I'm finding a way forward in business thanks to compassion and I much prefer the peace that this feeling brings rather than the fight.

To be honest, writing this book came as a bit of a surprise to me and just days before I was due to send this book to print I was asking myself (with a touch of criticism) "What the hell does EVOHE and this book have in common? Why are you even writing something like this…?" And then it hit me, like it had been staring me in the face the whole time: this book has the same core value woven all the way through it that EVOHE does.

Celebration of Life and Balance between Man Woman and Earth!

Part of me thought "doh!" and then another part of me just felt so thrilled to be offering both of these treasures to you right now.

When it came to my exploration of my cyclical nature, I naturally used my EVOHE products throughout my cycle - to soothe, uplift, nurture and optimise my experience of embodiment. Getting into my senses and connecting with my body can be a tricky thing since I tend to get so stuck in my head. EVOHE so beautifully brings me back to my body. It reminds me that my needs matter and it gives me the nurturing that I crave.

You will find my suggestions of which products work well in each of the seasons of a woman's cycle. I invite you to play with it for not only the women in your life but for you as a man. You need nurturing too and caring for your body is one of the quickest ways to loving yourself and recovering from the marks of fatigue that life can leave on us.

If EVOHE and this book can lend a loving light to you and yours in a time of struggle or crisis then I am fulfilling one of my deepest heart desires.

To make the world a better place by loving ourselves and each other - in the skin we are in.

In A Nutshell

Meghan Kurts (creator of EVOHE skincare) takes us on an off road journey into the cyclic nature of women, and boy what a ride! She openly offers her insights into navigating the menstrual mood swing, intimacy and relating.

No matter where you are at with the women in your life there is gold to be found here.

Finding balance and getting along better as humans cohabitating the planet together is the goal with this book. "This book has keys to unlocking some of the mystery that has had us baffled for years."

Including practical tools and suggestions that both men and women can follow, this book is a guide to the potentially bumpy road of 'that time of month' with plenty of directions and road signs along the way.

Clear examples and analogies, visual charts, videos and music links make the whole process an easy and comprehensive way to be "educated/initiated" into a woman's world.

Not only is there A Man's Guide, we have one for women too :)

A Woman's Guide - The art of the unwind.
Meghan has a free 5-page sneak peek of her up and coming book at evohe.com.au.

EVOHE also has a great Self Care page where you can take the Adrenal Fatigue test and follow it up with a Self Care Action Plan.

You will find heaps of other great resources here too.

Meghan also invites you to share in the conversation in both of her private facebook groups.

- (f) Nurture through the Cycles - for women

- (f) A Man's Guide Connect - for men

- (⊙) And, you are always welcome to connect with us via Instagram Meghan Kurts_Author.

Loved it! Great little read to open up consciousness and awareness of the cycle that has had me ducking for cover for frigging years.
Mathew Trede

Thank you again for your teachings, Meghan. It was a real honour, and, I feel, a lesson of compulsory significance.
William Frost

This stuff is GOLD. I can't express enough how life changing this has been for me and how much I feel it could benefit every man out there to know it!
James Brown

These insights have offered me a way to hold space and honour my woman while still staying on my own course. Following a woman's cycle makes me step up as a man and invest in our intimate connection. I'm definitely reaping the rewards from planting my seed.
Craig L

Introduction

Would you agree that all good things require a certain amount of attention?

I believe that understanding a woman's cycle is one of those things. I believe that understanding a woman's cycle is going to be mutually beneficial for all involved.

Do you ignore your body's messages and push through the pain? Do you numb yourself with various vices? We've all been conditioned to push through and often it is to our detriment. Women especially suffer from the 'push' due to their cyclical nature. The body needs rest in order to restore and recover, failure to do this results in burnout.

As much as men and women are different they are also very similar - pain is pain and human is human. As much as this book is focused on being a resource for understanding the cyclic nature of women it's also here for you. For you to make peace with your own 'yin' (feminine) qualities. To be gentle with yourself and give yourself compassionate understanding and reprieve from the 'push'.

By practising this information here with the women in your life, I hope that it spills over into your own personal practice of self-awareness and self-care, so that you can show up in your relationships whole and integrated - the best version of yourself being met by the best version of the women in your life. We need you, men, we want to trust you and surrender to your lead. See us and you will see the way.

Are you a partner in a long term relationship?
A father who wants to relate well with his daughter?
A brother, flatmate or work colleague who is baffled by the mysterious, everchanging nature of women?
Are you looking to open up to a new relationship that is based on authenticity, depth and connection?

Before we go any further, let me make one thing really clear... It's not your 'bad' for not knowing this and you haven't done anything 'wrong'.
(Although it may seem like it at times)

Bear in mind this is knowledge that has been around for a very long time. It was once considered the norm for a woman's cycle to be part of our society. Not a 'curse' and certainly not something hidden away.

It has been suppressed and forgotten hence there are a few generations that missed out on this information being introduced to them as a natural part of life.

At times along this journey you may also feel as if you are taking one step forward and two steps back. You may even find that you end up knowing more about a woman's menstrual cycle than she does. Yikes!

So in order to get there, we are going to have to go "off road" a bit. I'm hoping that by reading this you will pick up some practical tools along the way to put in your kit.

As well as the practical tools, it also seems like the most logical strategy for navigating your interactions with women.

"It takes the mystery and the guesswork out when initiating sex or other forms of communication".
Suzanne McQueen

A woman's menstrual cycle is her biology and it's not going away anytime soon. Put simply, we can't argue with a force of nature.
A woman's cycle is with her for her whole life.

Even if she has finished bleeding and has gone through menopause, she still cycles with the moon. Just like the tides.

So, I invite you to ride the waves brother!

Understanding a woman's cycle is the map to seeing a woman in her truest sense of self.
It is a key to unlocking and opening her.
And let me share a secret with you...she wants you to ☻. If you are looking for true intimacy, then this is foreplay at its realest.

I speak for myself and women as a collective when I say, "when we women reclaim the practice of following our natural rhythms we become empowered versions of ourselves. We show up authentically and are open to experiencing the connection and intimacy that we long for."

How To Get The Most Out Of This Book

This is not your average book. I like to see it as more of a resource that you can draw on.

There is a step by step guide through each part of a woman's cycle, with practical tips and suggestions.

Ideally, it would be great if you could bring to mind a woman who you interact with quite regularly. This way you will be able to relate this information to your own life and 'land the information in reality'.

The idea is that this benefits you directly and from a bigger perspective helps us all to get along better with each other!

As much as this information can be used as a map, it's best to treat it more as a guide.

I invite you to step lightly with compassionate curiosity and enjoy the treasure hunt.

So let's break it down.

First, we pair up the monthly lunar/moon cycle with women and their 28 day(ish) menstrual cycle.

Remember: that even if a woman has gone into menopause and stopped bleeding, she still cycles with the moon.

Then to keep it simple we break it up into 4 weeks in the month.

Each week represents a season. Winter, Spring, Summer, Autumn. The season is the theme or the flavour of the week. (The 'vibe').

Disclaimer: Please note - like anything within nature a woman's cycle doesn't always fit neatly into a 28 day package, nor will her moods reflect the seasons to a tee. As with nature there are infinite variables. It keeps things interesting to say the least. ☺

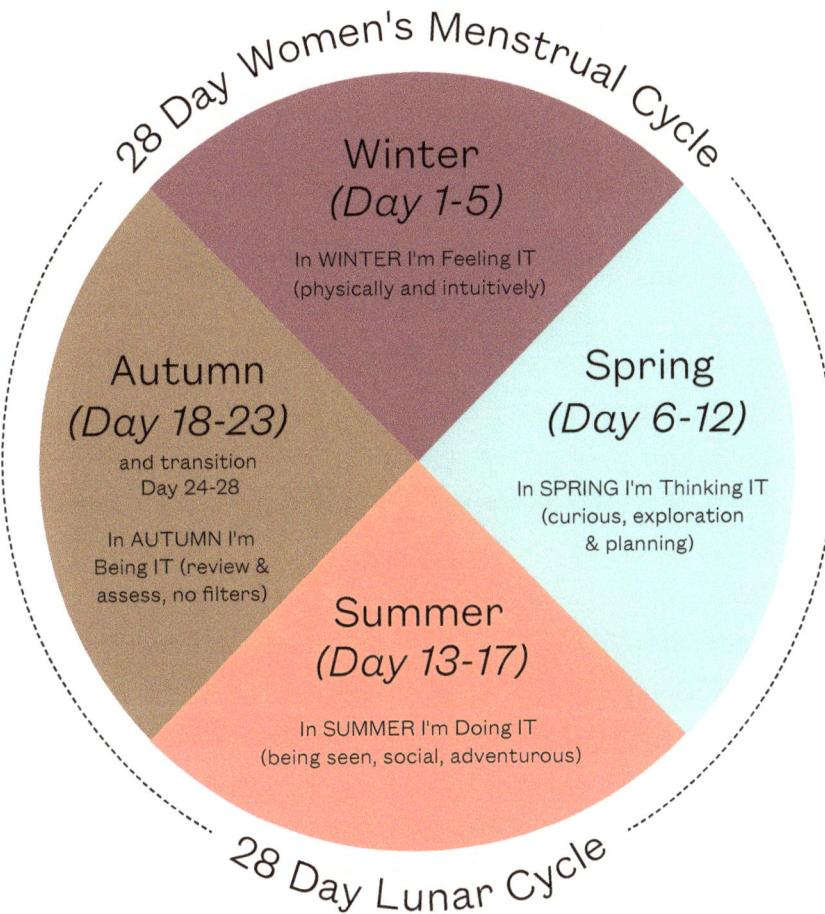

Let's Look At Your Why

(Might I suggest that you give yourself some time and space to do this process).

I invite you to bring a woman to mind that you have fairly consistent interactions with.

An intimate partner is good, but it doesn't have to be it can be a work colleague, sister, flatmate, daughter, it could be someone you co-parent with. With as much courage as you can muster, think about what seems to be the main issue or challenge you have when it comes to understanding her behaviour at different times in the month.

*please go easy on this - our intention isn't to make anyone or anything right or wrong or to solve the whole situation in one go - but we can certainly observe and take notice.

Lean in to what's not working. Give it a minute and some 'think music'. *Breathe. 'Go easy'.*

Now in just a couple of words, what is the crux of it - what causes the conflict?

Do you see a pattern? Breathe. 'Go easy on her & yourself'.

What kind of things do you currently 'do' in an attempt to keep things on an even keel?

Are there times when you still feel confusion or disconnection? *Breathe.*

Quick question: Do you see some women in your life pushing themselves to burn out and coming across like total crazies?

Knowing what you know about the situation, what do you think you can do? *Breathe.*

Don't worry if you haven't got a clear answer right now, just sit with the possibility that there could be a resolution.

My Why

The ideas that I put forward are not absolute, but if something feels right then give it a go, it can't hurt.

I have studied myself and countless women over the years – mainly so I can:

- Understand myself, my rhythm and a sense of my natural sexuality
- Keep my sanity
- Be an aware parent
- Run an ethical conscious business

I have come to the realisation that if I don't nurture my 'natural or wild self' I can not function in any kind of overflow out to the rest of my family or community. (that's a whole other story ☺)

My qualification is that I am a woman and this is my honest experience.

I have a genuine desire to relate authentically in all of my relationships.

I will openly share what I've learnt in the hope that it will
- Put out some fires and create some sustainable warmth
- Rebuild some of those bridges that we've burnt as a collective.

Esentially I just want us all to get along better. With a balanced foundation of compassion I believe we can solve/resolve pretty much anything.

My desire is that by communicating our needs we can...
- Heal the past;
- Transform the present; and
- Create the future

Filippa Araki. The Compassion Lounge

The Science (Short Version) ☺

A woman's cycle is approx 28 days - so it's not just the few days that she is bleeding. It is all of that and the rest!

A woman's moon/menstrual cycle affects her whole biology including:
- Her mental state;
- Sex drive;
- Ability to communicate.

As you know, for a woman to be able to have a baby her body has to prepare itself.

(It's actually quite phenomenal that an organ can shed and bleed like a woman's uterus does without it being fatal. So there is a lot of chemistry happening hormonally to build up the walls of the uterus and then shed them if an egg is not fertilised).

So, as a woman's hormones fluctuate, "she" fluctuates. Makes sense, right? It's natural.

Without conscious awareness and modifications to life, these fluctuations are known as The Hormonal Roller Coaster. And we can be left feeling completely out of control (men and women included).

Side note: it's not cool for women to blame hormones and use her period as an excuse to be a bitch. (Just sayin'). This is a time where we need to have compassion for both men and women.

We are all just doing our best with what we've got and we don't always have the filter of our "happy hormones" to ease us over life's speed bumps.

Note: For a deeper insight into the science of women's menstruation, see page 104, written by Sharon Maloney PhD.

If she were a car... the 4 stages

Winter	Days 1-5 (ish)	This is when she is bleeding and feeling her most vulnerable (even if she has her armour on and is pushing through), she would most likely rather stay at home cosy in bed.	**If she were a car** - the engine is cold The oil and filter are getting changed
Spring	Days 6-12 (ish)	She's peeking out from under the covers and thinking about getting involved with life again. She's planning.	**If she were a car** - the engines revving and she's warming up- ready to roll
Summer	Days 13-17 (ish)	Biologically, her happy hormones are optimising mid-way through at the time of ovulation - she's her most fertile and as with nature, she is 'out and about', 'she's taking action baby'.	**If she were a car** - she's at peak operating temperature just humming along
Autumn (Aka PMT) 	Days 17-(ish)	Tread carefully! This is where her hormones are dropping to their lowest up to the time she bleeds. This is usually the time when you see women (to be honest) at their worst. They can be intolerant and quick to temper to the point of such rage that it causes great pain for those around her and seriously burns bridges. It can also be a very confusing time because just 1 week ago she was in summer and ovulating and 'on top of the world'. She even may be quick to think that because of these 'mood swings' there must be something seriously wrong with her and given negative input by her family, friends and society, she might even believe that and go further into thinking she has a mental condition (which is often not the case). If anything she is hormonally depleted. That's all!	**If she were a car** - she's redlining and needing to back off the pressure so she doesn't blow - the sun is setting, best to take your foot off the accelerator and be aware of debris on the road. **SIDE NOTE - WARNING:** If you want to stay on the right track (and not lose your head) when you see a shift in her mood...DO NOT ask her if she is "getting her period"...(I'm sure those of you who have done that can verify the ramifications of this)

Cycles, Seasons & Archetypes

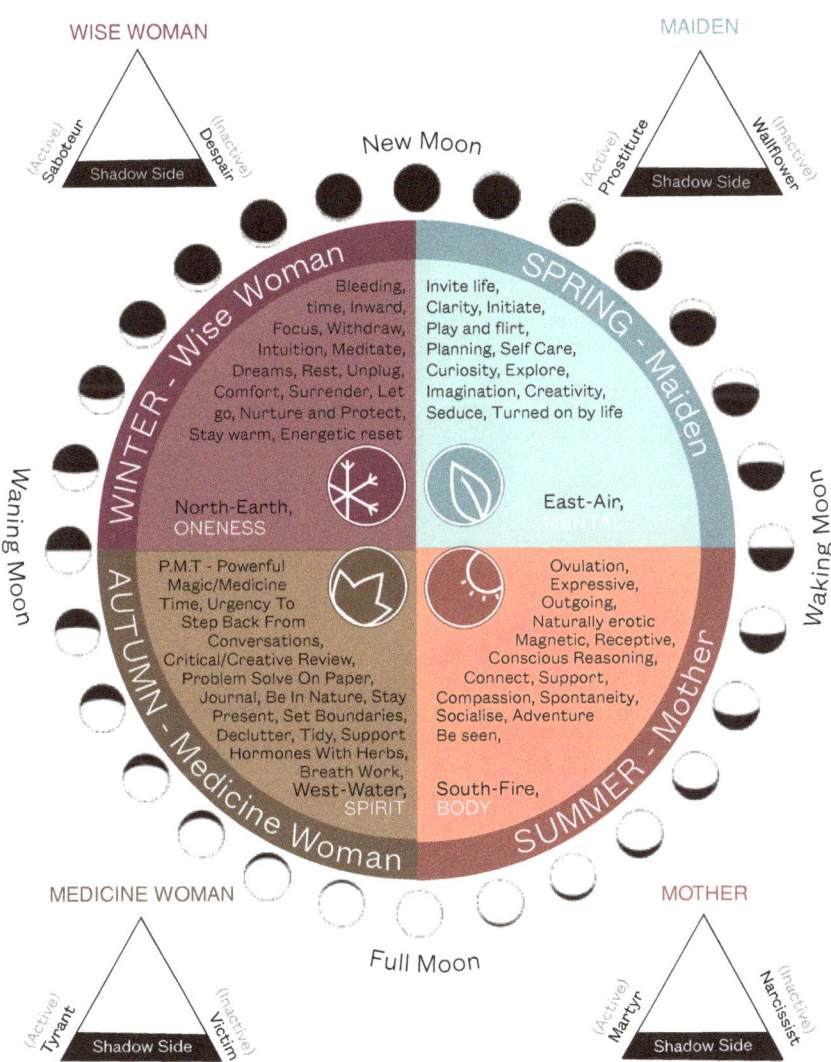

Archetype supportive contribution thanks to Jade Mason.

You will see with this chart that we are associating an archetype to each of the seasons.

The optimised or upgraded version is obviously what we are going for, but along the way we will observe the darker/shadow aspects.

These are to be embraced and our mission is to find the gifts they offer. Both active and inactive - conscious and unconscious.

There is no shame in the shadows.

They can seem scary at first but once they are given the loving attention they need, things tend to work themselves out.

Filippa Araki - The Compassion Lounge
Cultivate an undefended heart. Focus on what you love about your partner, co workers, children, friends and tell them. Tell them often. Ask for what you want in positive terms and not through criticism. Show the way by dropping your armour first. Undefend your heart and others' hearts will follow suit.

The Dark Side
(the mother aspect ready to receive the light of the father aspect)

This is when all the seasons blend into each other and everything just becomes a murky mess. A woman's happy hormones seem to be non-existent.

- She can feel lost and under a spell.
- She can feel like she has no real connection with her sense of self or her body.
- She can feel completely suffocated by what other people think and get caught up with proving herself.
- She can loop in cynicism and despair.
- She can be adrenally fatigued and verging on total burnout.

Many women feel this way for extended periods of time in their life, and you may see them go for months/years on end, wound so tightly that they could snap at any moment.

External conditions - typically include things like –
- Financial pressure
- Expectations in their careers
- Early motherhood
- Sleep deprivation
- Loss of a loved one
- Physical illness or injury
- Chronic stress from work/home environment.

It's not fun for anyone and it tests all relationships to say the least! These situations can contribute to women thinking they have mental conditions like anxiety or depression.

They often feel confused and don't understand what's come over them and why they are 'feeling' so much. I have described a time in my life like this as having no emotional skin.

(In fact that terminology was confirmed by a psychologist to me when my hormones tested to be chronically low, and I was diagnosed with Premenstural Dysphoric Disorder, aka Perpetual Autumn/Winter - at the time I was going through huge emotional stress and as a result, my happy hormones weren't able to find their way back up, as is usual with a woman's cycle... I felt like someone had stomped on my rose-coloured glasses and I was lost in the dark).

At this point I would like to acknowledge you for your courage and desire to support the women in your life. If you have brothers who are in the same 'boat' as you, reach out to them, have a conversation and support each other. This is a hero's journey and you don't have to brave it alone.
PS. - Thankyou for your willingness to even read this book.

Research has been done and trials are currently underway with psilocybin and other substances for trauma-based therapy. Although these options are yet to be legalized, Michael Pollen and Paul Stamets are respected 'thought changers' in the field and many people are experiencing significant recoveries from a number of issues. *See References

PPS - please check out the resource section - there are some amazing men and women out there doing amazing stuff to support us on this wild ride of knowing ourselves.
YOU ARE NOT ALONE

The Good News

The solution is pretty simple, but it's not often easy.

It's as simple as s l o w i n g d o w n.

Slowing down is the one simple thing that can make all the difference. Slowing down and listening to our bodies and getting to know their natural rhythm again.

I hear you: "try telling that to a stressed-out crazy lady who is constantly rushing around with kids, home and work life!"

Remember, we are dealing with a force of nature here. If we suppress it or resist it, it tends to leave a trail of destruction (you may already have first hand experience with this). I'm suggesting we try something different.

If we go 'with it' and invest our energy in the moments that really count, then there are likely to be more sunny days as time heals the wounds of the past.

Light can shine and direction and balance can be found; when life throws a curved ball at us we have something in reserve.

Risk/Benefit Ratio

- **Have you noticed that defying nature never seems to work out?**
There is benefit in non-resistance. Working with the hormones rather than against them...as Jade Mason (from Sovereign Woman) says, "resistance would be like saying to the storm - no you can't be here today!" You may just be surprised at what gifts come out of the stormy chaos.

- **Understanding your opposite/polar/feminine can open you up to your full potential as a man.**
At the risk of sounding a bit woo woo, learning about women in this way can also show you about yourself and your own internal feminine/yin nature - the idea is for all of us to find some equilibrium.

The benefit is that by supporting women to be in their balanced state they can then make space and be receptive for your true masculine state.

- **Consider it a work in progress – with payoffs along the way**
Know that this is the gift that keeps on giving and there can also be immediate benefits. You can use this as a guideline for happiness but it also has to be revised and explored on many levels.

Everyone has their own style and flavour so I would suggest being intuitive with it, noticing the signs and putting it into your own words or practice. I believe that practice of this will deepen our connections and levels of sexual intimacy, and I have a feeling we are all going to like that! ☺

- **Celebrate yourself as the Black Sheep**
You're taking a risk and making great change by doing so.
As natural as it is to follow a woman's menstrual cycle, it is not the 'norm'. In a way it feels like we are going out on a bit of a limb and taking a risk. Culturally we are in the groove of a 9-5 linear process - which asks women to push through and maintain a level of consistency - this is the crux of it, our lifestyles today are going against a woman's cyclic nature. Women are NOT linear, they are cyclic.

On top of this, many women suppress or control their menstrual cycles to suit their lifestyle or environment with various contraception methods & medication. Many of us are experiencing the backlash of this to varying degrees. **This is a pain point.**

Even though it can seem like hard work to start following a woman's cycle, I would say it's actually the path of least resistance - it's right in front of us and comes around every month, it's a really good tool that hasn't been utilised much in the past few hundred years, and can offer more benefits than we believed possible.

- **Get an Edge (upgrade) – optimise and experience flow state.**

The women and couples I see practising this are seeing real life tangible results. Admittedly it's still wobbly at times but we're finding a groove. A sense of belonging in our own skin. Some women may even turn to this knowledge of their cycles because it will give them an edge. Knowing where they are at will support them to thrive and be the optimized version of themselves in their careers, as mothers, in relationships and in their community.

Let's Get Back to the Simple Solution

SLOWING DOWN

To explore or practise any of this information, the first things a woman needs are space and support to slow down.

This will then give her the freedom and safety to explore herself and lean into some of the shadows that have been showing up in her life each month. From my personal experience, I would say that it is crucial for her to have the support of women friends, family, mentors and elders who she trusts and who she can call on when things get wobbly.

This leverage makes bearing the weight so much easier and the process so much quicker.

If she has been in isolation, exiled or cut off from these close connections, then part of that first step is to rekindle and build those supportive relationships.

There are many women out there offering services in this field as mentors/coaches etc.
See the resource section for some great practitioners.

When I committed to a 3 month course of mentoring and set that time aside each week for a one-on-one focused session, I found that I thrived and worked through the shitty stuff very quickly. I then felt that I wasn't burdening friends or family with all the details either. As well as this, sometimes when people are 'too close', the lines can get blurred and their opinions can confuse the situation.

So let's rip the bandaid off and see what we are working with here.

Self Love is a practice that requires some discipline to develop, just like doing your taxes or going to the gym. You have to put the time in & flex the muscle to get emotionally fit.

Tools For Her In Winter and How You Can Support

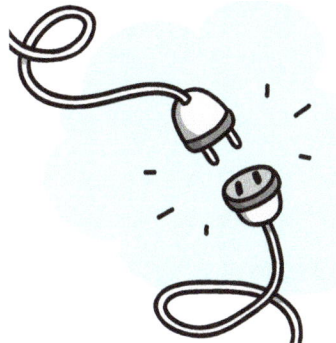

It's time for her to unplug... Put tools down and take an energetic rest

WHAT YOU CAN DO:
- Give her space to rest.
- Support her to set up the week with no big social engagements.
- Avoid big conversations decisions... no big family meetings!

It's time for her to step back from social conversations

WHAT YOU CAN DO:
- Ask her if she wants you to step up and support her in conversations.
- Be aware if she is struggling & step in.
  (This is your champion moment!)

It's time for her to take a long shower/ bath & soak in colloidal magnesium oil (breast massage is important too!)

WHAT YOU CAN DO:
- Offer to make dinner while she takes a long shower/bath.
- Give her the space & privacy, i.e. don't come in asking how long to cook the rice for!
  (& definitely don't try and get in the shower with her!)

Winter

It's time for her to wear extra comfy clothes & keep her lower back warm
WHAT YOU CAN DO:
- Heat up a wheat pack or put a hot water bottle in bed - this is you providing her so much bliss!
- Remind her she is beautiful in your eyes just as she is - she may be feeling bloated and not so beautiful...even a bit haggard.
- When a woman can feel loved even at her worst she can relax deeply and offer so many gifts.

It's time for her to meditate 3 days in a row (even for just 10 minutes)
WHAT YOU CAN DO:
- Give her space to allow this to happen.
- Share some playlists or podcasts that you think she might like.

It's time for her to only be around close circle people (as much as possible)
WHAT YOU CAN DO:
- Support her to do this if you can (sometimes women completely cut off from their sisters, when sisterhood is what they really need...gently encourage).
- A cup of tea and a chick flick can also do the trick 😊

Winter

It's time for her to sit quietly and simply listen to her wise woman...if inspired write from her wise woman

WHAT YOU CAN DO:
- If she feels like talking to you about this stuff...this is the best time to LISTEN.
- Listen & hold space - a lot of wisdom can come out of this. It's not a talking stick type conversation - listening is just listening!
- Don't try and fix anything.
- Don't come up with your own stories or me-too conversations (as tempting as it is). It's great you can relate but just try to LISTEN only.

It's time for her to say no to social events she doesn't want to go to (even if she has already said yes)

WHAT YOU CAN DO:
- Support her by making it okay to say no.
- Don't encourage her to push through. It will mean the world to her if she knows you are on her side and supportive of her 'no'.

It's time for her to notice her dreams & record them in a journal

WHAT YOU CAN DO:
- Support her by asking if she has had any dreams - and listen!
- Remind her to write them down.

Winter

It's time for her to say 'no' to strong caffeine & junk food
WHAT YOU CAN DO:
- Offer her the healthy version of comfort food.
- Check out Chef Cynthia Louise - she has all sorts of decadent healthy food ideas.

It's time for her to be conscious of energetically protecting herself (keep the portal closed)
WHAT YOU CAN DO:
- Be her guardian & protector (even just energetically).
- Hugs are so healing!

It's time for her to keep advice/feedback from others at a healthy distance & relook at it in spring/summer
WHAT YOU CAN DO:
- Hold back from offering advice/feedback.

You will get a much better response/outcome if you wait until she is in Spring/Summer.

It's time for her to spend time with herself & know how to make herself comfortable
WHAT YOU CAN DO:
- Ask her what you can do to help make her physically comfortable (the little details count!)
- Massage her body with colloidal magnesium - it will help ease muscles & cramping
- Take this time for yourself to do your own practices and have solitude time, to study or be.

When it comes to touch:

The right kind of touching during winter can set up the flavor of intimacy for the rest of the month. Now is not the time to grope her as she's bending down doing the washing!

Intimate, non sexual, or motive-free touch is so important to her while she's bleeding and feeling cold and vulnerable. Snuggle under a blanket on the couch, make her a cup of tea, nurture her now and reap the benefits for the rest of the month. She may be open to pleasuring you once she's feeling very warm, loved and nurtured. But let her come to that decision on her own.

Surprise her with long unexpected cuddles. Tell her she is loved and beautiful. Your warm hands on her belly and lower back will likely be well received.

I know this may seem like a lot and that you may have to really stretch yourself to accommodate all of these things, but I'm sure with consistent practice of this after a few months you will see a difference and it will be soooo worth it!

Now let's talk about sex - in the first few rounds of practising this supportive role and developing a deeper connection with your partner, it is best not to have expectations. Soon enough she will begin to thaw out and her Winter bleeding time will be a time that she may naturally want to love all over you sexually.

She may be satisfied to honour and pleasure you, because she will likely not feel like penetrative sex, but happy to give you an orgasm. It could be a time where it's all about you sexually.

NB: Sometimes it can be a relief for women with heavy cramps to have an orgasm but it is more of a functionary thing rather than an erotic thing. She may prefer to pleasure herself at those times. Stay open.

Find the ultimate Winter Woman nurture pack at

e v o h e . c o m . a u .

We've had some experience with this and have a feeling it's going to be well received.

Spring

Tools For Her In Spring and How You Can Support

It's time for her to have an at-home facial, massage or get her nails done!
WHAT YOU CAN DO:
- Have a facial or massage with her - try Lomi or Kahuna for something different
- Book her a nail appointment.
(It's a great gift she normally might not spend money on, but would secretly love!)

It's time for her to play with a good girl friend
WHAT YOU CAN DO:
- Encourage her to have some girl time - away from you
(It's so important for women to have their own playmates)
- This is your time to play too - set up a mates date & enjoy some bro time.

It's time for her to look at the months ahead and coordinate her calendar (give her space to do this alone)
WHAT YOU CAN DO:
- Get on board when she's in a planning mode
When women have all these things sorted in their mental spheres, they can really let go and trust the process of life. Tidying up the head stuff will help to get into her body and be willing to play and feel more flirty.

Spring

It's time for her to sit down and make a plan, write a list or an inspired action mind map

WHAT YOU CAN DO:
- Allow her to do this alone at first - if you show openness she will probably love to share.
- Let her iterate the entire picture before giving feedback - or even better, wait until she asks you for suggestions before you offer your piece.

It's time for her to get up earlier this week

WHAT YOU CAN DO:
- Make it fun with some playful encouragement.
- Join in!
- Roll straight out of bed onto a yoga mat and do some light stretching together.

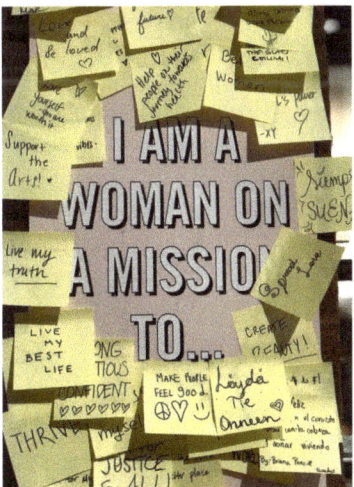

It's time for her to initiate something she has wanted to do or that needs resolution

WHAT YOU CAN DO:
- If you know of something - bring it up in a light way without any expectation.
- Say out loud what skills you observe in her (it will mean so much).

Spring

It's time for her to hula hoop, hopscotch, jump rope or blow bubbles in the garden

WHAT YOU CAN DO:

- She needs to reconnect with her playful maiden, so any gifts that you know she loved as a young girl...bring it back!
- Get colourful with drawing or painting
- Buy her an adult colouring-in book - it's something she probably won't buy herself, but if gifted, may just love it!

It's time for her to have a nice hair treatment
As you can see there's lots of girly pampering going on! This is so she can be ready to fully express herself in Summer. Supporting this process will be well worth it. All of this Spring preparation is like foreplay for Summer!

WHAT YOU CAN DO:

- Let her know that you love that she is pampering herself AND that she is beautiful as she is too - the idea is that pampering is nurturing & fun, we don't want her to become a slave to the 'beauty myth'.
- i.e. The Beauty Myth - the shadow side to women preening themselves based on culture, telling women they are not enough, they are too old & 5 kilos too heavy etc.

It's time for her to speak with a mentor/elder whom she admires & trusts

WHAT YOU CAN DO:
- Learn together - this is always an option for you too! Ask questions.

It's time for her to be flirty & curious about what she likes sexually... speaking about a fantasy is a safe & helpful way to discover what she likes

WHAT YOU CAN DO:
- Get involved but also be aware that too much mentalising of sexual desires (e.g. porn) will densensitise and take the true feeling out of a sexual exchange in real life.
- Explore the idea of her natural sexuality with openness and innocent curiosity. There may be past hurts that still need healing.
- If you can treat her more like a virgin exploring her sexuality at this time, she will begin to open and trust you. If she shows you a body part - follow her lead and go to that part. (e.g. wrist, neck and wherever that leads). **Kissing is important.**

Spring

It's time for her to do a mini cleanse/detox
WHAT YOU CAN DO:
- Support her or join in!
When her body feels good/healthy she definitely feels sexier.

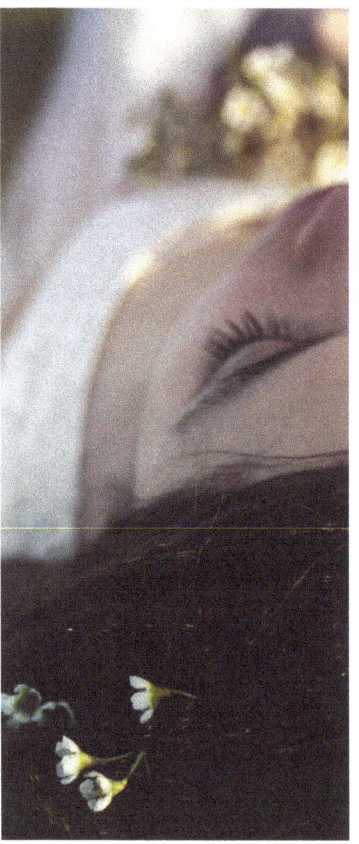

It's time for her to really listen to her body & get out of her head
WHAT YOU CAN DO:
- Help her by offering to place your hands on her body (with no expectation or goal focus). Simply just to ground and breathe.
- Start with a head masage and then move one hand onto her forehead and then the other onto her heart and start to sync your breathing.
- Once she relaxes a little, move your hands to her heart and lower abdomen.
Simply breathe together.
- If she likes her feet being rubbed, this is a good time aswell.
(help to get her grounded - out in nature is always a good remedy).

Spring

When it comes to touch:

The virgin. If she's all loved up from all the warm snuggles from winter she'll be in overflow and wanting to play, flirt and explore with you. Approach with curiosity and compassion. Keep assuring her and letting her know she is safe in your love. If you can delay penetration, foreplay alone can be a mind blowing experience.

Touch can be sexual, but try kissing her neck, rubbing her thighs, and even if she's asking for sex, try to prolong foreplay and kissing as long as you or she can handle it.

Excite her with long seductive kisses and firm touch. Show her that you desire her.

Surprise and delight your Spring Woman
with our Spring nurturing pack.

evohe.com.au.

Designed just for her, we think she will love it.

Tools For Her In Summer and How You Can Support

It's time for her to dance under the moon
WHAT YOU CAN DO:
- Get involved
  See her and adore her for whatever she shows you.
- It's time for her to show up & be seen in all her glory.

It's time for her to dress up & be a bit bolder than usual
WHAT YOU CAN DO:
- This is when you can plan those special nights out.
- Get involved!
- Express your admiration and show your appreciation, don't be shy.

It's time for her to meet new people
WHAT YOU CAN DO:
- Encourage this and get involved
  This doesn't mean you have to be there for all of these new meetings - giving her space in this way will earn her trust and make her want to come home to you even more.
- Autonomy is a powerful presence and ecouraging each others soverignty is super sexy!

Summer

It's time for her to do something spontaneous - watch this space
WHAT YOU CAN DO:
- Get involved! Surprise her.
  This is the time where she's more likely to surrender to the flow of life and say YES!

It's time for her to wear her hair out more or experiment with a new style
WHAT YOU CAN DO:
- Encourage her!
- Be generous with your praise.

It's time for her to be creative (and a bit naughty) with food - YUM!
WHAT YOU CAN DO:
- This is when you can indulge a bit together.
- Get into holiday mode and enjoy the reprive - even if it's just for a day.

It's time for her to have an adventure! creating content that she can share :)
WHAT YOU CAN DO:
- Be there with her.
- Encourage her creativity.

Summer

It's time for her to consider playing out a fantasy
WHAT YOU CAN DO:
- Set it up & be there for it.
- Let her have it or develop it more by communicating about it.

It's time for her to get sunshine on her yoni (vulva)
WHAT YOU CAN DO:
- Help her go for it - it can shift things greatly.
This is not as bizarre as it sounds! Many midwives actually recommend it! It's just a little hard to pull off in some neighbourhoods.

It's time for her to let go of the martyr and victim patterns & reclaim her sovereign empowerment
WHAT YOU CAN DO:
- Sit back and watch it unfold. If she slips back into old patterns just know the process takes time.
- Encourage her to be unapologetic and bold.

It's time for her to be brave and have a big conversation that she knows will require a lot of compassion
WHAT YOU CAN DO:
- Show up for this and bring whatever you need to share to the table, this is the time.

Summer

It's time for her to break the Disney spell of the 'perpetual maiden' and be authentically who she is

WHAT YOU CAN DO:
- Applaud her.
- Give her reassurance that she is beautiful and you love her for who she is without the makeup.

It's time for her to get shit done

WHAT YOU CAN DO:
- Step out of the way if there is a project she really wants to get done.
- Or step in and offer her your physical support.

It's time for her to be aware of what she is committing to, with the knowledge of what she has the capacity for

WHAT YOU CAN DO:
- Be careful not to encourage her to extend herself too much in this time. When Autumn hits, she could end up feeling overwhelmed from over-committing.

Summer

When it comes to touch:

If you have both been honouring her cycle for sometime, Summer can be full of epic sex. Now is the time to take her dancing, tell her she is sexy, SEE her, and hold on for the ride. Quickies, experimenting, and wild sex on the kitchen bench are all now a possibility. Let her lead but show your enthusiasm. Be available for anything.

Relish in her and celebrate your relationship. Tell her how much you appreciate her!

Make big plans. Create something friggen awesome together. This is the whole point of being in an intimate relationship. CREATION. Whether it's a baby, a new project, an adventure or giving to a cause you both believe in, now is the time!

> EVOHE have designed a pack especially for the Summer Woman - watch the beauty unfold right in front of your eyes with this gift
>
> evohe.com.au.

Autumn

Powerful Medicine Time (PMT)
Depending on where she is at and the levels of her hormones, it could go in two ways - Victim/Tyrant or Medicine Woman.

Tread carefully as you are entering sacred ground. Ask permission to enter. In her Summer phase she has been extremely magnetic - she either has the capacity to roll with the momentum or she will begin to feel the overwhelm of all that she has been creating. She will instinctively start to discern and prepare herself to shed.

If it's not nurturing her and supporting her then she may just let it go - the shadow side of that would be to slash it, smash it, burn it to the ground. If you see this happening, simply step back and give her space. Remember DO NOT ask if she's 'getting her period' if you want to keep your head.

See if you can spark the Medicine Woman in her. She may be able to roll with the flow of the seasons and be in a position to hold space for magic. Her cauldron is simmering, so ask her if you can be involved in the magic or if she wants space. Be totally okay either way - beware of your feelings being potentially hurt if she seems to 'reject' you - it's actually not the time to take it personally. Be aware that anything she may point out is still valid, even if it comes out a bit irrational or emotional.

Autumn

Tools For Her In Autumn and How You Can Support

It's time for her to change gear and slow down as the summer energy/hormones begin to drop

WHAT YOU CAN DO:
- Allow her to have space & allow yourself to have space too.

It's time for her to support herself with herbals and supplements

WHAT YOU CAN DO:
- Support her/remind her to take them.
- Join in on the herbal supplement thing. It will be good for you too

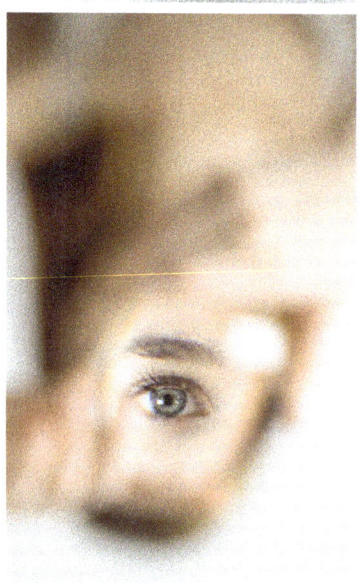

It's time for her to do a creative review on her life

WHAT YOU CAN DO:
- Don't jump in on it with her (she is doing her own critical analysis)
- Hear her out, but don't try to invalidate what she is noticing by trying to:
   a. Fix it
   b. Disagree with her to try and make her feel better
   c. Defend yourself if it involves you - protect yourself by all means by letting her know that you will take it on board/sleep on it and come back to discuss it when you can.

Autumn

It's time for her to problem solve on paper
WHAT YOU CAN DO:
- If she's looping, don't engage in the conversation - suggest she write it down in a journal or talk it out with a girlfriend.

It's time for her to journal all the yucky stuff
WHAT YOU CAN DO:
- Buy her a beautiful journal as a gift (it's not often something women will buy themselves).

It's time for her to 'prepare' the house for winter - tidy, declutter & cook
WHAT YOU CAN DO:
- Help her do this - this is a good use of all that energy, plus she needs this to feel safe
- Do some of the yucky jobs that have been put off - especially the ones you know she doesn't want to do while she's in her Winter phase (e.g. kitty litter, taking out rubbish etc.) *From the consistent feeling of safety & support you will see the happy woman you fell in love with again.*

Autumn

It's time for her to acknowledge what makes her wild/crazy

WHAT YOU CAN DO:
- Give her space and distance on this one 😌
- Don't take her delivery personally - however keep in mind that what she says is likely to be valid
- If you have the capacity, hold space for her by honouring her thoughts & allow the energy to release so that it doesn't explode later.

It's time for her to use all her tools to stay present and not burn bridges

WHAT YOU CAN DO:
- Support her (check out the support section). This is the time when she really needs your unwavering presence.

It's time for her to research herbal medicine & study some kind of self development

WHAT YOU CAN DO:
- Encourage and remind her of interests that you might have noticed she has. Support her to spend time on these personal endeavours - they are important.

Autumn

It's time for her to focus on breath and learn further breath work

WHAT YOU CAN DO:
- Help her to discover!
- 10 conscious consecutive breaths a day can make all the difference. Do it with her.

It's time for her to book a self Development/mentoring session

WHAT YOU CAN DO:
- Support her to make this happen. E.g. look after the kids, gift it as a present etc.
- Validating her spending time or money on self development will mean the world to her.

It's time for her to head out and be in nature as much as possible

WHAT YOU CAN DO:
- Get her out into nature and just walk - it will soothe her nerves like nothing else!
- She may resist at first but hopefully will thank you later.

Autumn

It's time for her to yoni steam
WHAT YOU CAN DO:
- Support her!

It's not as weird as it sounds. See here: evohe.com.au/lets-talk-about-yoni-steaming/

It's time for her to have a sacred space in her home or a small altar of her precious things
WHAT YOU CAN DO:
- Support her to have some space in the home that is just hers...and you really honour it! (e.g. don't leave any of your stuff in there) And make a space or zone for yourself too, if you don't already have one.

It's time for her to harness the PMT (powerful magic/medicine time) energy to optimise her life
WHAT YOU CAN DO:
- She can turn that intensity into good use and you can turn up for the sex magic (this is a whole other story!).
- Encourage time in nature and anything creative.

Note from Jo Brown: For Medicine Women to be met, the boy has to step up and become the man - moving beyond fear of death - it is the time for him to bow at her throne in the truest sense.

Then the king is born and he knows how to control life by embracing death.

When it comes to touch:

Often men can feel very confused when just yesterday she was riding you like a wild sexy beast and today she seems to flinch at your touch.

Take notice of when the switch flips. It's no longer ok to tweak her nipples as she's getting out of the shower.

But also know, SHE IS NOT REJECTING YOU.

Autumn sex can be a deep, spiritual experience but you must find the way in.

Warm oil massage, candles, ritual, and sacred space, help her to know that you just want to be intimate with her even if sex is not a possibility.

This can lead to incredible sexual experiences where she feels like she can let down all her insecurities and go primal with you, because she feels loved and seen for who she is.

This is potentially a time where all the primal sexual energy stirred up in the Summer phase can 'land' and be utilised in sex magic (that's a whole other conversation).

EVOHE have carefully designed a bold and beautiful pack for your Autumn Woman to let her know you are there for her and are also able to give space - check it out -

evohe.com.au

QUICK GUIDE FOR WHAT TO DO IN EACH SEASON

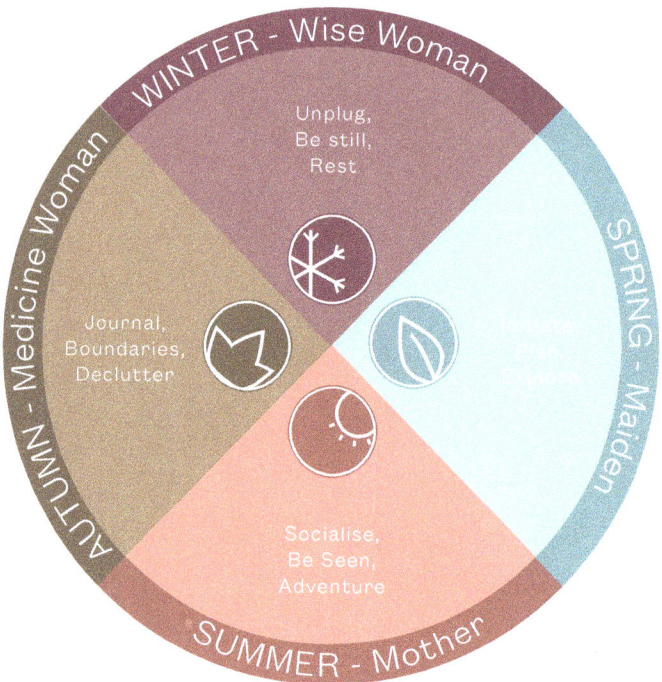

I've discovered a benefit to being at total burnout with an empty cup - because to truly start filing my own cup I realised I had to empty it first. Empty it of people, activities, and things that weren't nourishing me. Starting from square one with just the basic necessities for survival - healthy food & water, safe space/shelter, quality sleep and support from people who want the best for me was a game changer. My social circle became very small if nothing at all and I went into a kind of self-enforced exile or deep recovery. I was able to gather back all of my scattered energy and use it to recharge myself instead of fueling others (that can come later when we are authentically in overflow).

Following my cycle along with a daily practice of self nurturing was literally a lifeline for me when I was in a very dark place. I felt like nothing was working and everything was pointless - the small sustainable steps to recovery happened through simple self care and EVOHE was at the heart of it.

evohe.com.au

Embodiment:

An embodiment practice is essential for women when it comes to understanding their 'monthly flow' and navigating their emotions. It's also an essential key to feeling aroused and being intimate with our partners.

Embodiment means that there is an awareness of feeling in the body and from that space, we take our lead and navigate life rather than life and circumstances ruling us.

So many women are desensitised by life circumstances and cultural pressures that there is a general numbness.

For them to feel any sensation it has to be at a higher level of intensity.

This causes stress on the nervous system and could even be said to be traumatic to the body and heart, especially when someone is unconscious of what their body is truly asking for or needing.

Having a simple embodiment practice assists people to re-sensitize themselves to their bodily sensations and their feelings; from here we can heal old wounds and simply recover from the onslaught we have put our bodies through. It is only then that we can get on with feeling the pleasure and juiciness of being alive in these bodies.

I believe this process requires time and a lot of self-awareness. There is no real short cut, but a skilled Somatic practitioner can certainly assist with both the mental and physical aspects of trauma in our bodies.

Plus check out my spotify 'embodiment' playlist **Meghan Kurts Forrester** or **megforrester**

And see Appendix for Exercise suggestions for a woman as she follows her cycle.

The Yin & Yang of it all

We each have YIN and YANG qualities within us. Essentially Yin is feminine and Yang is masculine. When it comes to navigating the cyclic nature of women, having this knowledge can come in handy.

A woman traditionally may be more YIN skewed and a man may be more YANG skewed.

It could also go the other way, where a man is more YIN and a woman is more YANG. It also just depends on where and what is happening at the time.

But either way you slice it, for there to be balance, each individual requires both YIN and YANG in a ratio that complements.

The chart on the following page comes directly from my interpretation of Toko-pa Turner, Author of Belonging and facilitator at Dreamwork with Toko Pa, she is a source of deep inspiration for me and it is with deep respect and humility that I offer my interpretation here.

The Inner Marriage:

YIN Qualities:
- emotional nature
- feeling
- Intuitive
- spontaneous
- dreams
- inspiration
- source of growth
- unseen
- daydream
- relax
- be without doing
- trusting inner knowing

Underdeveloped Yin:
- Workaholism,
- Relentless pursuit of ambition
- Compulsive busyness
- Completely identified with the outer world - shallowness
- Loss of feeling in the body - desensitised

Overdeveloped Yin:
- Drowning in emotion
- Overwhelmed by everything
- Difficulty making decisions
- Irrational

THE WAY THEY DANCE TOGETHER:

Where YIN is diffuse moonlight - YANG is direct sunlight.
YIN receives by withdrawing - it enters by 'going in'.
Where YANG enters by going forward and penetrating.

YIN's intuitive direction gives guidance which understands the interconnected needs of the whole.

YANG builds and works towards making it happen and supports the intuition of YIN, which serves the culture. Yang articulates the vision and walks it in the world
YIN is the gestation of the idea - receiver of the dream.

YIN is inclusive of both, whereas YANG is this or that. Right or wrong. Either / Or.
YIN expands by having a surge of emotion where YANG fearlessly stands by and supports with strength and ability to focus.

Yang says you are a changing ocean and everything is contained within you.
I will stand by you without judging or criticising YIN's emotion as hysterical. YANG will consider it all valid and passing and be unwavering in the strength to NOT get caught up in the tides of emotion but to discern what is valuable and leave the rest.

YANG Qualities:
- rational
- assertive
- mind
- intelligence
- independent
- discerning
- economic
- politics
- law
- science
- direction
- focus
- steadfast
- backbone
- follows through on the plan
- manifests into form supplies order
- logical

Underdeveloped Yang:
- Invalidation of own voice
- Inability to move out of potential
- Too many ideas
- Can't move forward / fear of moving forward
- Depression
- No clarity or direction

Overdeveloped Yang:
- Domineering
- Controlling
- Unyeilding

The Inner Marriage

There is an interdependent dance - a noble beauty in the pursuit of balance within.

When two beings come together with this intention it complements both parts within the whole and then there is an overflow of the most beautiful kind.

In order for us to fit together in harmony, we have to contain within ourselves a piece of the opposite.

When there is an imbalance within us that is not conscious we tend to look for that need to be met by a partner - this feeds into all kinds of patterns and conditions.

If you look closely at yourself you will see your own pattern playing out and how you look for deficiencies in yourself to be met by another.

This most often is a recipe for certain failure.

You can acknowledge areas that you don't shine in and can admire that quality in a partner but it is more of a complement to your already wholeness rather than someone supplementing you.

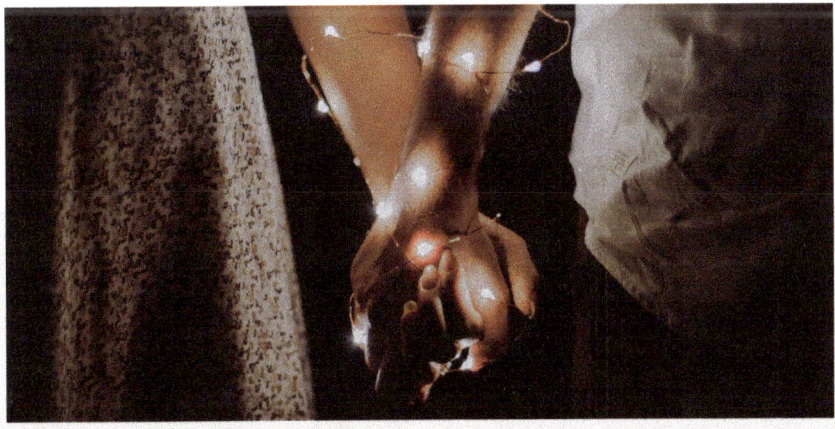

A Question We Hear Often From Men:

How can we support a woman who doesn't have connection with herself and her cycle?

A good place to start is by knowing her Love Language.

This shows that you are being attentive to her needs and will build trust and begin the thawing out process.

There are many wonderful tools for women to connect with their cycle these days - the best way for you to point in any direction is through your actions and your behaviour.

Ps.- if you would like a sneak peek at my upcoming book **A Woman's Guide - The art of the unwind,** go to **evohe.com.au**

How To Speak Your Partner's Love Language

Which Love Language?	Communications	Actions	Avoid
Words of Affirmation	Encourage, affirm, appreciate and listen actively.	Send an unexpected note, text or card.	Not recognising or appreciating effort.
Physical Touch	Non-verbal use of body language and touch to show love.	Hugs, kisses, cuddling.	Inappropriate or uninvited touch.
Receiving Gifts	Thoughtfulness, make your partner a priority.	Give thoughtful gifts and gestures. Express gratitude when receiving gifts.	Unenthusiastic gift receiving, forgetting special occasions.
Quality Time	Uninterrupted and focused conversations. One-on-one time is important.	Create special moments, take walks and do small things with your partner.	Distractions when spending time together. Long time without one-on-one time.
Acts of Service	Let them know you are wanting to help, to lighten their load.	Make them breakfast or dinner. Go out of your way to help with chores.	Lacking follow-through on small and large tasks.

Men Have Cycles Too!

An addition to all of this information about Women's cycles, is that Men have cycles and archetypes too.

We can complement each other and support each other to be the best version of ourselves.

This is another fascinating subject - one which I am very interested in understanding and developing.

Currently, Asher Packman and other male friends of mine are going into deep conversation about this and I'm sure we will come out the other side of it with some helpful insights!

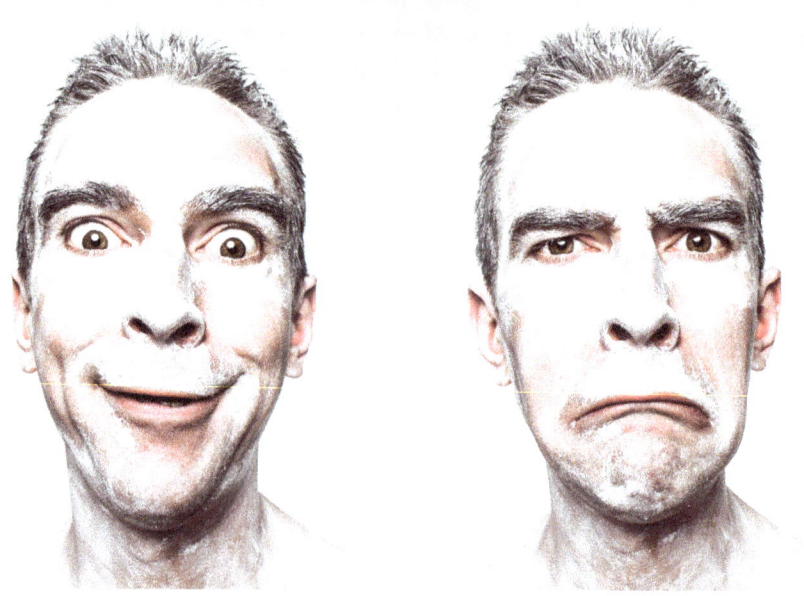

Feel free to connect with other men in our private facebook goup **A Mans Guide Connect**.

MENS RESOURCE PAGE
Men who've got your back

Resilient Leaders Foundation
James - Jamesgreenshields4@Gmail.com
www.mesilientleadersfoundation.org

Mankind Project
Recommended by James Greenshields
www.mankindproject.org

Nicholas De Castella
Recommended by James Greenshields
www.nicholasdecastella.com

The Fifth Direction
Asher
asher@thefifthdirection.com.au
www.t5d.com.au

Karma Wellness
Cam Fraser
kamawellnessperth@gmail.com
0424 692 009
www.facebook.com/kamawellnessperth
www.instagram.com/kamawellnessperth

John Wineland
www.johnwineland.com

Alistair Mckinnon
Conscious Directions
alistair@consciousdirections.com.au
www.consciousdirections.com.au

mens well being
www.menswellbeing.org

In Summary
From Meghan

Wherever you are at with the women in your life right now, know that trust is earned from the little things. It all adds up. Just by you showing an interest in women's biology and emotions shows a loving awareness that women don't often see in our culture. Your generosity to show up for her armed with this knowledge is a true Mature masculine moment. Providing a safe container, listening to her perspective, letting her know that her feelings are valid and that they make some sense to you is one of the greatest gifts I can imagine a woman receiving. It doesn't mean you have to agree with it all or understand it all. But just that you are present and willing is what allows the trust and the deepening to occur. Remember how deep the iceberg goes when you look under the surface.

I believe many women are only showing you a tiny if not backwards version of themselves; that they themselves feel as if they don't even know who they are on any given day. Many women are being what they think they should be, have been taught to be or are manufactured to be by our society. The conditioning runs deep and it's a bit of a tangled mess.

When I see the false eyelashes, makeup that looks like a mask, cosmetic injectables, boob jobs and labia surgery, I see how lost we have become. Men and women have been conditioned to think the skinny blonde (a.k.a Barbie) is what's desirable. And yet when I speak with men in real life they don't want their daughters or sisters or lovers to look like that nor do they want them to assume the positions represented in porn. Men, help us break the spell we are under. For so many women when it comes to sexuality they don't even know what their authentic responses are in the moment. She follows your lead and is conditioned to please. There may be surface level satisfaction but not the depth that I believe we all naturally desire. On an intimate relational level, however, you can have all of the versions of a woman you crave. Yep, you can have it all…by complementing a woman's cyclic nature with your own masculine depth you can have it all.

The loving nurturing wise woman, the virginal maiden, the hot sexy mama and the magical goddess. She longs to be a vessel that feels like home to you - somewhere that you can land and that she can surrender to. With your awareness will come her responsiveness. It may be like a slow thawing out process, it may open a can of worms - there may be an intense backlog of emotions that come to the surface. Remember you're not alone. Life on this level of awareness requires support, a wilderness guide and as many tools and resources that you can get your hands on. There are many paths and it's your job to find what works for you, adapt and modify and enjoy the unfolding.

Now that you know this…what will you do?

RESOURCES & REFERENCES

PRACTITIONERS: Intuitive, Compassionate and Amazing - something to connect with and experience for yourself

- Fillippa Araki. *Conscious Communication.* www.compassionlounge.com
- Angela Fitzgerald. *Birth Your Truth.* birthyourtruth.com
- Jo Brown. *The Balance of Masculine and Feminine Within.* sacredunionmentor.com
- Astro Allstarz. *Modern Cosmic Intelligence via Astrology.* astroallstarz.com
- David and Judith Weinstock liminalsomatics.com
- Moira Williams. www.pureheartcentre.com
- Michaela Boehm. www.michaelaboehm.com *(awesome podcasts on her site)*
- Dr Steve Katz. *Infinite Potential Centre.* infinitepotentialcentre.com
- Moira Bradfield. *Naturopath - specialising in Womens Health and Fertility* moirabradfield@hotmail.co.uk 0400838586
- Lissa Gavins. *Health Kultcha - specialising in Womens Health.* info@healthkultcha.com.au 0422 793 351
- Kyle Laz. *Herbalist.* www.facebook.com/klazich
- Tanya Miles. *Herbalist.* 0401 444 453
- John Wineland. www.johnwineland.com
- Philippa Kelly. Psychologist philippakelly@hotmail.com

ONLINE COURSES

- Toko-pa Turner. *Dreamwalking: A Course on Dreams* toko-pa.com/dreamwalking-a-course-on-dreams-by-toko-pa-turner/
- John Wineland

GREAT READING

Non Fiction -
- Toko-pa Turner. (2017). *Belonging: Remembering Ourselves Home. (my absolute favourite)*
- Alison Armstrong. (2013). *The Queen's Code.* www.queenscode.com

- John Gray. (1992). *Men Are From Mars, Women Are From Venus.*
- Gary Chapman. (2013). *The Five Love Languages.*
- Naomi Wolf. (2002). *The Beauty Myth.*
- Naomi Wolf. (2012). *Vagina.*
- David Deida. (1997). *The Way of the Superior Man.*
- Amara Charles. (2011). *The Sexual Practices of Quodoushka: Teachings from the Nagual Tradition.*
- Caroline Myss. (2001). *Sacred Contracts.*
- Margot Anand. (2017). *Love, Sex, and Awakening: An Erotic Journey from Tantra to Spiritual Ecstasy.*
- Miranda Gray. (2009). *The Optimized Woman: Using Your Menstrual Cycle to Achieve Success and Fulfillment.*
- Ayelet Waldman. (2016). *A Really Good Day. (excellent for understanding Menopause)*
- Sharon Moloney. (2018). *Activate Your Female Power.* www.sharonmoloney.com
- Toni Weschler. *Taking charge of your Fertility.* tcoyf.com
- David Schnarch PhD. *Secrets to a Passionate Marriage.*
- Doug Gillette. *King, Warrior, Magician Lover.*
- Robert Bly. *Iron John.*

Fiction -
- Jean Auel. (1980-2011). *Earth's Children Series.*
- Starhawk (1993). *The Fifth Sacred Thing.*

ON YOUTUBE

- Sasha Cobra. (2017). www.youtube.com/channel/UCwM7aT7wUvIs_LImMEIaYKg/
- Alain de Botton. (2016). *On Love.* www.youtube.com/watch?v=v-iUHIVazKk
- Alain de Botton. (2008). *The School of Life.* alaindebotton.com/the-school-of-life/
- The Art of Manliness. (2018). *Exploring Archetypes With Jordan B. Peterson.* artofmanliness.com/articles/podcast-335-using-power-myths-live-flourishing-life/

- 12 Rules for Life. www.youtube.com/watch?v=x9QHIEbO4OM *(20 minute version)*
- Nicole Daedone. (2011). *Orgasm: The Cure for Hunger in the Western Woman.*
  www.youtube.com/watch?v=s9QVq0EM6g4
- Shayla Ray. (2018). *Sacredness (The Blood Song).*
  www.youtube.com/watch?v=iKx85ka917s
- Brett Hayes. *Tri Breath.* tribreath.org/
- Tara Brach. *Compassion and Empathy.* www.tarabrach.com
- Mama Manon. *Aware Parenting.*
  mamamanon.com/playful-parenting-for-cooperative-kids
- Sera Beak. (2013). *Red Hot and Holy: A Heretic's Love Story.*
- Charles Eisentein. (2016). *Rex Brangwyn: Building Erotic Intelligence.* charleseisenstein.net/podcasts/new-and-ancient-story-podcast/rex-brangwyn/
- Brene Brown. *Supersoul Sessions: The Anatomy of Trust.*
  brenebrown.com/videos/anatomy-trust-video/
- Michael Pollan. (2018). *How to Change Your Mind.*
- Eckhart Tolle. *Ego relationship vs. real love*
  www.youtube.com/watch?v=rG3XIIjIw2A
- Lucy Peach The Power of the Period
  www.youtube.com/watch?v=9Yj5BaqXFNI
- Why you will marry the wrong person. *Alain De Botton*
  www.youtube.com/watch?v=-EvvPZFdjyk

HEALTHY EATING

- Chef Cynthia Louise www.chefcynthialouise.com/
- Caroline Scott. *Nutritionist 0404 141 714*
- Casey Conroy www.funkyforest.com.au, www.othersideart.weebly.com

PERIOD TRACKER APPS

Eve | Glow | Clue | Period Tracker

SPOTIFY PLAYLISTS BY MEGHANKURTS

- Check out my playlists for each season
  open.spotify.com/user/megforrester

PODCAST

- Michaela Bohem
- The Concious Locker Room
- Marion Rose. Aware Parenting
- Oprah Super Soul Conversations
- Juliette Allen. Authentic Sex
- Esther Perel. Where should we begin?

Practitioners

Filippa Araki

Filippa Araki (compassionlounge.com) is passionate about sharing the tools and insights of Compassionate Communication that have transformed her inner and outer life. Through decades of personal questing and growth, Filippa gained personal experience of the radical difference that conscious communication skills make in relating to self, others and the environment. By developing an inner space of self-compassion and understanding, we bring more love, acceptance, and integrity to all our relationships. Mother of two, long term educator, and an internationally certified trainer in Nonviolent Communication (NVC), Filippa supports others' journeys towards living more lightly on the Earth in connected and sustainable communities.

W: compassionlounge.com
F: @compassionlounge
E: connect@compassionlounge.com

Chef Cynthia Louise

Hello! I'm Chef Cynthia Louise.

I'm a published co-author of 3 international bestselling cookbooks, with Dr Libby Weaver; REAL FOOD CHEF, SWEET TOOTH STORY & REAL FOOD KITCHEN... I'm super proud to work alongside this incredible human who has taught me so much when it comes to how we absorb food.

For years I have worked in exclusive Health Retreats where I was limited to the number of people I could support. And now I can through my 24/7 online cooking classes where I guide you in your kitchen from mine to create meals that serve your organs.

I'm also the creative food director of the global brand GENIUS CAFE, building 50 cafes worldwide. It's a joy to train the next generation of chefs on how to look after themselves and their customer's ultimate health with what they are serving on the menu.

I have my own healthy cooking retreat called nourish a 5 day conscious cooking journey in Bali. A hands on retreat where we go deep into the world of plant based cooking.

I am an international speaker and presenter on wholefood cooking and eating the way nature intended us to be when it comes to living a thriving energetic life.

What makes me crazy is all the confusion out there about what to eat! I want to bring some clarity and realness to your table. I'm a working mum and a businesswoman. I know how hard it is to find the time to nourish ourselves and our families.

I am here to give you everything you need to make your own extraordinary everyday food, from scratch, using real ingredients.

I share this knowledge with humans all around the world. Real people. Real ingredients. Food as nature intended. Food is such a special gift, and I love its ability to bring people together and to nourish us on all levels – I love it!

I am a big supporter of women's health and wellbeing through the way

I teach about how I like to cook and eat (taking the bullshit out of eating really).

Chef Cynthia
www.chefcynthialouise.com

Jo Brown

Aussie born, with a corporate past life, Jo has been on a humbling journey of self enquiry and service for a quarter of a century. She's a mum and a traveller at heart.

She was trained over 28 years ago by an esoteric physiotherapist in bodywork and the anatomy of human energetics while exploring yoga, dance, feminine sensual rituals and meditation.

She supports women through transformational retreats and programs supporting feminine wellness leadership throughout Australasia. She lives in Ubud Bali.

"my greatest joy comes from whispering women's magic out of rememberance back it our hearts and hips again through everyday rituals."

"I offer workshops, trainings , mentoring and one on ones online and in Bali and Australia. I also offer Bali Healing Escapes for individuals and small groups in Ubud which are intuitively designed programs for my clients highest evolution.

sacredunionmentor@gmail.com

Sharon Moloney

Dr Sharon Moloney is an author, speaker, women's health practitioner and therapist. She guides women to find, reclaim and embody their sacred female power, especially around their fertility, menstruation and birthing. She also enjoys working with men to support them to understand women. Her mission is to restore the sacredness of the female body in order to create male female balance. Sharon believes that every woman has inside her a unique contribution to planetary healing and evolution, and that our bodies are our most intimate connection with Nature. Her book, Activate Your Female Power,is a guided journey into that intimate connection, regardless of life stage or fertility status.

Her contact details are:
www.sharonmoloney.com
sharon@sharonmoloney.com
M: 0437 825 564.
www.facebook.com/miraculousmomentsbirthing

Moira Bradfield

Moira Bradfield, Intimate Ecology M Acu, B Nat, PhD Candidate.

Moira Bradfield, founder of Intimate Ecology clinical and education services, is a Naturopath, Acupuncturist and educator with over 18 years clinical experience. She has a passion for helping people experience optimal health in sustainable, connected and sensible ways.

Clinically she has a niche interest in recurrent vaginal infections, optimal vaginal and genitourinary health, hormones and the vaginal microbiome (the bacteria and microbes that reside in the vaginal cavity).

Moira holds a Bachelor of Naturopathy Southern Cross University, a Masters degree in Acupuncture from Southern Cross University and is a PhD Candidate at Griffith University in the area of the vaginal microbiome and recurrent vaginal infections.

In addition to her role as a Naturopath Moira has lectured in Naturopathy, biosciences and nutrition both overseas and in Australia.

She maintains a busy private clinical practice in Miami Queensland (Intimate Ecology) and is also available for consultation via teleconferencing platforms.

Pages:
www.intimateecology.com.au
www.instagram.com/intimateecology/
www.facebook.com/intimateecology/

Moira Bradfield
M.Acu, B.Nat, Dip TTM, MANTA, AHPRA (Acu)
Ph: 0400838586

Kyle Laz

For the past 10 years Kyle has dedicated his life to deeply researching and exploring plant medicines and their application to body, mind and spirit. He has visited many of the key sacred sites of England and Europe, gaining spiritual and practical knowledge from his experiences. This has allowed him to understand the diverse relationships between western health and spiritual concepts and be able to offer holistic healing. With a strong focus on the five elements, he continues to develop practical processes to recognise, ground and integrate profound, mystical experiences.

His passion for holding a space for transformation and healing continues to expand, and the profound wisdom Kyle offers can be experienced through community sound immersions, online group programs, one on one health coaching or long distance healing. He works and trains with a range of modalities including Reiki 1, 2 and Master Teacher attunements, Acutonics, Massage, Flower Essences, Crystal Healing and Chocolate Ceremonies (a fusion of herbal wisdom, sound and chocolate). His sound healings bring deep connection to the self through a range of instruments including 9 Quartz Crystal Singing Bowls, Tibetan Singing Bowls, Flutes, Didgeridoo, Pan Drums, Shakers, Vocal chants and singing.

kylelaz.com/contact/

Vanessa Montgomery

Vanessa Montgomery - a.k.a Astro All-Starz - is a professional astrologer, writer and author of Star Power: A Simple Guide to Astrology for the Modern Mystic. Resident astrology expert at Glamour.com and Whimn.com.au, Vanessa's writing has been featured internationally from Vogue U.S to Vice Broadly.

Utilizing the ancient art of astrology, planetary and lunar cycles, counselling and various change modalities, Vanessa facilitates clients and readers to better understand themselves, others and life.

While happiness and success are important goals, ultimately her work is aimed at enlightenment and seeing past labels to the oneness that unites us all. She encourages each and everyone to trust their inner voice, and listen to their heart to light the way.

Her personal motto is Free your mind, Own your power, Create your world.

Vanessa
0425234659

Casey Conroy

Casey has been an Accredited Practising Dietitian and Nutritionist since 2012, and a Yoga Teacher since 2006. Her passion is helping women to free themselves from body dissatisfaction, disordered eating, and weight preoccupation. She also loves working with pregnant women, new mums and their bubs. She believes that we can learn a great deal about how to best care for ourselves from observing nature's cycles, from ancient traditions, and from listening to our bodies.

In her work she draws upon her parallel life as a yoga teacher of 10 years; her childhood growing up exploring forests, picking bush foods, watching her Chinese-Malay mum incorporate Traditional Chinese Medicine into everyday cooking and life, and exploring remote corners of Australian wilderness with her meditation-addicted dad; her past life as a veterinarian and environmental researcher; and her lived experience with and full recovery from disordered eating.

In her spare time Casey loves to write – she is a feature columnist for Living Now magazine and an avid blogger. She enjoys painting, napping (every mum's fantasy), crafting, trying not to kill plants in her gardening attempts, sageing the hell out of her home, herbal medicine, 80's glam metal, prop-heavy yoga, campfires, travel, and exploring forest trails with her family.

Infinite Potential Centre

The Centre for Empowerment Wellbeing Growth and Evolution Infinite Potential Centre is a Wellness, Personal Growth and Development Centre committed to assisting people to develop revolutionary new strategies to work with emotional, mental, chemical and physical stresses of life both past and present.

We do this through working with your nervous system's physical and energetic structures helping to improve the connection between body and mind. This work increases awareness and flexibility, enabling the individual to cope with and respond more productively to life's challenges.

The Centre does not aim to fix anything or treat anything. We work on the premise there is nothing broken, that everything the body presents is an opportunity to utilise for growth and development.

We offer you the space to change your physiology, change your perspective and change your behaviour to enhance the quality of your life.

www.infinitepotentialcentre.com

Angela Fitzgerald

Angela is a gifted birth healer, writer and speaker. She helps women heal from unexpected outcomes of childbirth, miscarriage and abortion. She also sees what is often overlooked in women's lives and returns women home to their core feminine essence and radiance. She leads women to the light within them, no matter what darkness they have been through. She is a much loved midwife of the heart and soul of women everywhere.

Love,
Angela Fitzgerald
Birth Spirituality and Healing Coach

angela@birthyourtruth.com
www.birthyourtruth.com
+61 422 450 096

Brett Hayes

Brett Hayes is a regenerative practitioner based on the Gold Coast of Australia. As head coach of the breathing, mobility and body sculpting program called TriBreath, Brett teaches people from all walks of life and age, how to improve and maintain their body mobility and respiratory fitness.

Using three specific breathing rhythms and various techniques when you walk and run, you learn how to "tune your body up, by timing your body up to your breath!" You'll move easier, breathe deeper, walk taller and run faster!

Link to Brett's teaching platform is... www.tribreath.org

Jade Mason

Jade is a modern day mystic who provides support for the modern individual to be empowered in their relationship with self and others.

She offers relationship coaching, mindfulness mentoring, sexual & menstrual education, circles, workshops, space holder training, yoga, bodywork & tarot readings. With a combination of ancient wisdom teachings, consciousness expansion practises & modern day support structures, Jade's mission is to empower individuals to thrive and live their best life.

Jade is the founder of the Sacred Women Mystery School which is a support and education space for both men and women to be supported & nourished with feminine wisdom and nurturing.

Her aim is to provide a cutting edge education and community building platform where individuals and families can be supported to live in accordance with natural law and reclaim sovereignty in all areas of life, love and relating.

www.jademason.co

David and Judith Weinstock

David and Judith Weinstock are both international trainers in Nonviolent Communication (NVC). Through the lens of their original work, Somatic Consensus, they share practices for learning NVC from the inside out.

David is a somatic coach, master goldsmith, Aikido instructor, musician, and author of Becoming What You Need: Practices For Embodying Nonviolent Communication. Judith is a counselor, master chef, author and musician, and has run her businesses through consensus decision-making for four decades.

Judith and David, along with eight other families, co-founded an intentional community in the US where they have raised their family since 1990. Their community is thriving and now in its fourth generation. Together, David and Judith lead trainings in schools, communities, organisations and businesses around the world.

www.liminalsomatics.com

Moira Williams

Moira is a caring, supportive Emotional and Spiritual Healer, Metaphysical Counsellor and Meditation Teacher with over 20 years experience. Her ability to remove negative energy and channel powerful Healing Energy enables you to regain Balance, Love and Truth. Her counselling techniques encourage self empowerment, clarity and a sense of peace.

Moira offers private consultations, in person, over the phone or Skype. Retreats are also available along with workshops and classes at the Pure Heart Centre.Moira began her Spiritual awareness journey with her Diploma in Anatomy and Physiology,Diploma CounsellingDiploma in Transpersonal Counselling,Certificate in Meditation/Self Discovery,Reiki 1 & 2 (practitioner), Therapeutic Massage, Astrology and Numerology.

Salacia Waters Gold Coast, Queensland
Get Directions m.me/pureheartcentre
Call 0402 257 456

Michaela Boehm

Intimacy Teacher, Lineage Holder, Author, Wild Woman, Animal Lover.

www.michaelaboehm.com

About Meg

Mother and CEO of EVOHE Skincare, Meghan knows that life is a juggle and that we need all the practical tools we can get our hands on just to stay afloat.

Maintaining her sanity as a solo parent has played a big part in Meghan reclaiming her awareness of her cycle.

She believes it reveals the true depth and potential of herself as a woman.

Meghan shows that through a consistent practice of Self Nurturing and Self Connection we can fill our cups and overflow into the rest of our lives and greater community.

By living true to her cyclic nature she finds herself thriving and optimizing her energy both in relationships and business.

Meghan lives a simple life focused on showing up as the best possible version of herself every time.

She lives in the lush Gold Coast hinterland and is inspired by the men and women in her life who have come before her and who see and love her for who she is no matter what kind of day she is having.

Meghan loves being out in the elements at dusk and welcoming in the evening stillness, practising sitting with what is and then applying it in her life. She hugs herself regularly and believes that women should regularly wear skirts so that they can easily pee out in nature! :)

Winter *Spring* *Summer* *Autumn*

APPENDIX and Contributing Articles

Appendix 1

Exercise

Exercise has both its dark and light aspects for both Men and woman.

People can push themselves to beyond burnout through exercise or they can thrive and feel amazing.

If we would like to move or exercise in a way that is not only good for our bodies but also for our hearts and souls then we must consider 'why' we are doing it.

Looking at your 'why' is always a good start in gauging if the exercise you are doing is a help or a hindrance to your psyche.

Do you do it because you feel you should? Because that's what other people are doing and say you should be doing?

Do you do it because you think you are fat and there isn't really a filter for that on Instagram..?

Or do you do it because you know you feel better and happier when you get some movement happening or that your knee is starting to hurt because you know you are carrying too much weight and you would like to look after yourself better? What I mean by this are you looking after yourself not out of shame but out of love and care for yourself?

If you are forcing yourself out of shame then I would suggest stopping everything and having a little sit down with yourself and really getting to the core of it before you take up any physical exercise.

Yes, there are so many physical advantages when we exercise but these should be more of a bonus or side effect.

If we can all exercise not out of guilt but for the joy of it, the pleasure, fun, community etc., then we will get so much more out of it as a whole feeling being. For women, in particular, choosing their 'type' of exercise in relation to their cycle is very important.

I would suggest easing off anything that 'pushes' them beyond what feels right for their body at any time.

Women really need to let go of the expectation that they are going to be the same every week, because we just aren't. Exercising by following the cycles or seasons for women can mean a whole new regime and a whole new happier woman.

Winter Moves

When it comes to movement during winter it's best to keep things on the low down.

Stay as close to the earth as possible. Simply sitting on the grass and doing some stretches is about all you need to do. Gentle forward bends or child's pose can be great, but always listen to your body's wisdom. Instead of pushing your body into something, try leaning into it instead.

Seated or supported restorative yoga postures can work wonders for reducing cramps and discomfort.

If there is a lot of discomfort, gentle walking can shift things around - even just for your headspace.

Curling up on the couch or in bed is always a wonderful option - if you are doing this, then give yourself the extra support by having a pillow under your legs, or if you're on your side, then a pillow between your knees.

Spring Moves

We just wanna have fun in spring, nothing too serious or structured is ideal.

Jumping in pools with friends, hoola hooping, dancing and running around being silly at the beach are all legitimate exercise. We've just come out of a potentially dark few days and we want to keep it light.

A class here and there is fine but nothing too strenuous is best. If yoga is on the cards then opt for supported postures using a block, bolster or the wall - even though we are feeling so much better after our bleeding time we need to be mindful to go easy on our bodies as we come out of the cave. (Beware: it's tempting to overdo it because we are feeling so much better and then we end up in deficit - use healthy restraint).

Summer Moves

Go for it with the cardio and get your blood pumping.

It's great to feel and know where your edge is but don't get so close that you go over it. This never helps, if anything it sets you back. So enjoy the energy that your body feels and run with it.

Team sports are great at this time too or partnering up for some good sessions with a mate.

Consider the adventurous side of you and be bold with your moves this week. Jump out of a plane, rock climb, take the kayak out in the waves, do an epic bush walk that you've been building up to...you get the idea.

Autumn Moves

We move into more of a solo action time, don't be surprised if team sports aren't your thing this week.

We may find ourselves rearranging the furniture, which is excellent exercise but on our own, the whole house can end up in quite a state.

A good solid walk/run out in nature is always best to clear the Autumn tension.

In the early part of Autumn, we can handle fairly strenuous classes, but as Winter draws near, be very mindful of slowing down the pace.

Appendix 2

The Science - Longer Version
by Sharon Maloney, PhD

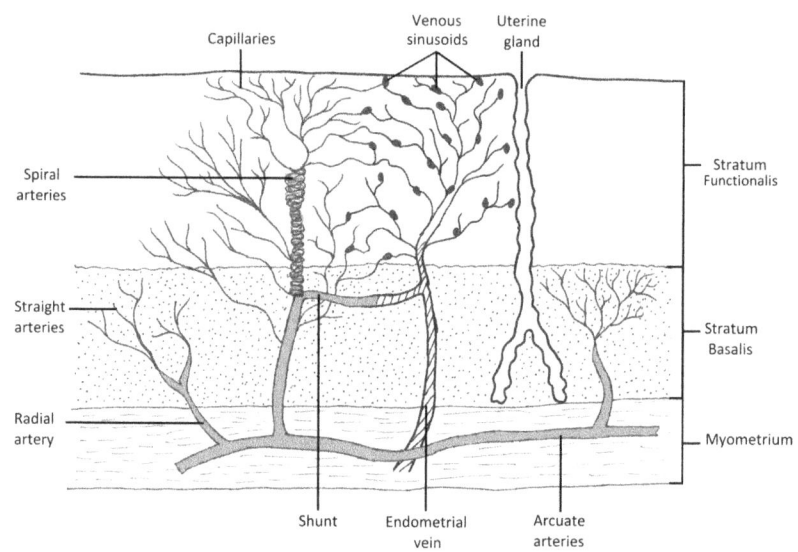

Diagram by Caitlin Moloney

The biology of the menstrual cycle is nothing short of spectacular! It's really a marvel of nature happening inside a woman's womb when she's menstruating.

There's an enormous amount of intelligent, creative activity going on deep below the surface and if you understand what's actually going on physically during this time, you'll have a greater appreciation of what your woman is experiencing and also of what she's doing on behalf of humanity. This hidden contribution rarely if ever gets acknowledged, even by women ourselves. And yet it's enormously significant and valuable.

As you're about to find out, menstruation is a huge expenditure of energy! It involves a lot of physically demanding work, which many women know intuitively, yet don't really understand.

So let's take a guided tour through this mysterious inner landscape to give you a chance to really appreciate its amazing design and the incredible amount of building and rebuilding that happens during the menstrual cycle.

The Physiology of Menstruation
Why do women menstruate?

The womb lining, because of its vital role in sustaining a fertilised egg and hence a pregnancy, has to be in mint condition, so it gets discarded and rebuilt every month.

Photos inside the womb reveal a lush, deep red surface, which many women find surprising. This lush redness is created by the womb's extraordinary blood supply, which has some very unusual qualities.

To truly understand the process of menstruation, we need to delve into this remarkable blood vessel system which has some pretty astonishing design features and powers of growth.

The womb lining is made up of two layers:
1. The functional layer (stratum functionalis) which is shed during bleeding and then regrows during the cycle
2. The base layer (stratum basalis) from which a new functional layer grows at the end of each bleed

Inside the muscular wall of the uterus, the uterine arteries branch into several arcuate arteries (the arcuate is part of the pelvic bone), which then branch out into radial arteries that supply the womb lining.

Up to this point, the blood vessel branching is similar to anywhere else in the body.

However once the radial arteries reach the womb lining, an altogether different and completely unique arrangement takes over.

It's very cool! Here's what happens.

The radial arteries branch into two different kinds:
1. Straight arteries, which are short and divide to form capillaries in the base layer
2. Spiral arteries, which are longer and coil upwards to supply the functional layer, where they form capillaries near the womb lining surface

Spiral arteries are the key to understanding menstruation. Highly sensitive to the hormones from the ovaries, they have a unique structure and function seen nowhere else in the body.

As the name suggests, the spiral arteries twirl upwards through the growing functional layer in a dense, coiling pattern that looks like springs.

This design cleverly delivers a much richer blood supply to the womb lining.

Amazingly, this coiling happens because the spiral arteries grow at a much faster rate than the surrounding tissue and as a result, they have to continuously compress themselves more tightly into the available space.

That's an impressive feat of biological engineering!

A second unique feature of spiral arteries is that they grow little 'shunts' which bypass the capillary network at the womb lining surface and instead connect directly with the veins deep below the surface.
Normally arteries end in capillaries in the surface tissue, which is where the veins take over. The 'shunts' are a special adaptation intrinsic to the shedding process, as you'll see.

The brilliance of the design doesn't stop there.

Alongside the spiral arteries, there's an extensive network of specially modified veins in the functional layer, with sinuses where the blood pools.

These venous lakes or sinusoids are thin-walled, allowing large molecules like proteins and blood cells to pass between the blood and surrounding tissues.

Blood flows slowly through the venous lakes, allowing it more time to pool and thereby providing a richer nutrient absorption, an ingenious strategy with obvious advantages for a burrowing embryo.

The amazing fact to comprehend is that this elaborately constructed network of blood vessels, shunts, glands and venous lakes completely disintegrates during menstruation, along with the entire functional layer.

That is remarkable! Imagine if that disintegration happened inside your liver or your lungs or your heart. You would be seriously unwell. And even more amazing is that our wombs do this incredible work every month, over and over again, for three to four decades.

Maybe this is why menstruation is sometimes called the Blood Mystery. It's certainly a mysterious capacity to regenerate an organ's tissue on a regular basis.

After the bleed is over for that month, the base layer begins rapidly reconstructing a new functional layer in response to hormonal signals from the brain and the ovaries.

Stimulated by rising oestrogen levels, the cells on the surface of the womb lining begin to heal and regrow, and a whole new network of blood vessels starts to rebuild.

The spiral arteries spring up, growing out to resupply the new functional layer, while the uterine glands enlarge as they begin secreting their juices. In less than a fortnight, the womb lining has completely regrown and is ready for another potential fertilised egg to burrow in.

Impressive powers of regeneration!

Around the time of ovulation, the womb lining is at its thickest. The spiral arteries extend and coil to their maximum, ending in a dense capillary network close to the surface of the womb lining.

Progesterone then transforms the newly grown functional layer into a juicy, succulent surface, from which swollen glands release a sugary substance. Much like what happens in the vulva during sexual arousal, the entire blood vessel network and surrounding connective tissue of the womb lining swells with fluid.

The lining is now poised at the fullness of its potential: lavish and lush, engorged with spiral arteries and miniature lakes of nutrient-rich blood, this is how it becomes that vibrant red colour. Laden with life-sustaining fluids, its entire surface is bursting with readiness in anticipation of a burrowing embryo.

If none arrives, what an anticlimax after such an extravagant preparation! About 12 days after ovulation, the womb lining loses its hormonal support and prepares to shed.

The process by which this happens is a marvel of biological engineering! The sudden drop in progesterone and oestrogen causes a shrinking of the functional layer so the surface cells begin to die off.

As they do, tiny organelles within the cells known as lysosomes (which are full of strong digestive enzymes) are released and the functional layer begins to self-digest in readiness for the menstrual flow.

This shrinkage also means the spiral arteries have to coil and compress even further, and this in turn, restricts the blood flow to the functional layer.

As a result, the spiral arteries begin to kink and buckle, and the surrounding tissue starts to die off.

Because of the constriction in the spiral arteries, most of their blood flow is abruptly redirected through the special 'shunts' into the veins and sinusoids.

With the lining already weakened, this sudden blood redirection creates a rupture of both sinusoids and capillaries, which then spreads throughout the functional layer. The affected area begins to detach and at the same time, the smooth muscle beneath the base layer begins to contract rhythmically to assist the shedding process.

So begins the menstrual phase of the cycle, with bleeding for anywhere between two and seven days. Some women bleed every cycle for four or five days with a good flow on all days.

Others have two or three days of heavy bleeding, followed by several days of lighter flow or spotting. Generally, a bright red flow of at least three days indicates healthy fertility. Average blood loss during each period is about 30–40ml, with 80ml considered a heavy loss.

As you can see, there is great deal of complex, intelligent construction, breakdown and reconstruction in the confined space of the womb lining during menstruation!

You can now appreciate the enormous amount of vital life force energy expended by women in this creative biological activity.

Sacred Blood

Perhaps the most important thing for you to know about menstruation is that it's a deeply sacred process. In Western culture, we don't have any ceremonies to mark the spiritual significance of menstruation.

Yet in Indigenous traditions like the First Nations people of America and

Australia, and some parts of India, menstruation is regarded as a time of naturally heightened openness to things of the Spirit.

This is why women were relieved of their normal duties and went into seclusion – so they could receive vital information that would benefit the whole tribe.

It's mainly the hormonal state during menstruation that renders women more porous to the invisible world of Spirit.

And it's important for all of us to remember that every person who has ever existed in the history of our species began life in that blood.

Yes, menstrual blood is literally the cradle of life and that also makes it sacred.

I hope this description of the biology behind menstruation enables you to appreciate Nature's design as it occurs inside the wombs of the women in your life.

And that you'll be inspired to honour them for what they're doing during this special time of such deep shedding and transformation.

Some people believe that menstruation created the world. I'm inclined to agree.

Appendix 3

The Light of the Ever Loving Gardener

I haven't always had a great relationship with the female members of the human family. This can more than likely be traced back to when I was growing up. My mother worked three jobs from the time I can remember.

Where was my father you may ask; the male? Well he decided to leave my mother for another woman when I was about six months old and my eldest sister was around three. As such I had limited contact with males and my feelings about women were they weren't there for me! And that was true. My mother wasn't available a lot of the time. For the harsh reality was she had to work in order to buy food and provide shelter for her children. My father gave nothing and offered nothing.

When I left school and started a trade, my perception of what women were and represented didn't really make things any better. Unfortunately, as a young apprentice I was exposed to an array of pornographic shows that occurred deep down in the bottom carparks of the office buildings we were erecting (if you'll excuse the pun).

These shows with women playing the starring roles, in reality, laid waste to the wonder and beauty of the woman! The truth is, these shows only created more separation and instilled fear and inadequacies into my young, pliable receptive mind about my role and relationship with women.

I believe it was an understandable reaction considering these shows graphically displayed (among other things a young boy or girl shouldn't be exposed to) the insertion of "let us say tools-of-the-trade" into every available orifice and entry point found upon the female body.

An Introduction to Harmony through Destruction
In my early twenties, I fell in love with a woman more than I was in

love with my own life. The desire was strong and lucky for me she left me with a shattered and broken heart. The pain was excruciating and almost unbearable! But all so necessary for the role all males and females alike are offered! Why? Because the walls of sadness, isolation and despair that I'd built around my heart in my early years were very well fortified and only an explosion of mass proportion could possibly have any chance of "bringing that wall a'crumbling down!"

And down it came!

Time passed (like a couple of years) and I was blessed to experience the waters of relationship with other women and with their help and every now and then tears, I got myself up from my knees and the weight of heart broken despair lifted. Within those relationships, I was always aware of the possibilities and consequences that came when males and females connect. That's how come you and I are here. With the possibility of creation always being present, my past experience of being abandoned by my father was an experience I didn't wish to pass onto anyone. So I started looking at my thinking!

For He is The Sun and She is the Earth

Being an avid gardener, I always showed a keen interest to study of the seasons, the moon cycles and even the tides. It was by working with nature that helped me grow beautiful and nourishing produce. From the preparation, the sowing, the maintaining and the growing, all became clear as to how I could help create a better world.

I would see myself (the male) as both a gardener and a planet. For the male is like the Sun is to the Earth.

I would see my partner (the woman) as both the soil and a planet. For the woman is like the Earth is to the Sun.

As a gardener, I know if I wish to partake of heavenly produce, my role and continuing action is to nourish the soil. Protect the soil. Water the soil. Feed the soil. Feed the Earth! For that's what the woman is! The woman is the Earth that gives birth to more life!

I believe my role (as the male) is decreed by Nature upon any potent gardener. That is to nourish, warm and feed the soil. For the male is like the Sun is to the Earth!

So long as the male shines his light upon the Earth, the Earth (the woman) can flourish and provide nature's bounty.

It is by this way of thinking that I have and continue to experience far-reaching possibilities of growth. When the Earth (the woman) is going through stormy weather, emotional weather, and goodness gracious the clouds of heaviness can be full and engulfing, all the Sun has to remember is to keep on shining. For He (the male) is not the Earth... He is the Sun! The seasons are always changing on the Earth and probably always will.

I believe as the givers of light and warm is the role we males are designed for! If it wasn't so, we wouldn't be the seed-carriers who seed and fertilise the soil. It is by this way of thinking, that in my life I am provided with the most beautiful women who love and adore me as I love and adore them.

It's this way of thinking that has given me the opportunity to experience the love of family both with my partner and our children but this love has grown exponentially to also encompass the greater human family.

They say, "as a man thinketh in His heart so shall He be". I believe the path to a fulfilling relationship with a woman is to hold true and act upon the simple thought to feed, water and shine light upon the soil.

Sure there'll be dark days on planet Earth, but that is not the burden for the Sun to carry. Know if the Sun holds true to His own light and keeps on shining (knowing He is not the Earth), eventually the Earths clouds of despair will dissipate; the hurricanes blowing debris his way will settle and the scorching fires from the volcano's mouth will subside, leaving only fertile soils yearning to bathe in the light of the ever loving gardener.

Appendix 4

Sacred Union – The Energy Science Of Yin And Yang
by Jo Brown Sacred Union Mentor

Men's and women's brains are not the same and neither is our biochemistry.

We operate through fundamentally different lenses when it comes to relationships.

Dr. Louanne Brizadine explains in 'The Female Brain" that women possess a language and emotional centre in both spheres of the brain while men possess one only in the left hemisphere.

Women on a average are better at both picking up on others' emotions and expressing their own. Reading emotional nuances in others is part of a woman's hardwiring. Men move, think and feel in a linear fashion from point A to point B. Women are hardwired to assess and respond immediately from our emotional language centres. Men are not. It does not mean men are incapable of expressing their emotions, rather that their brain structure is designed for action - primarily to protect, and if necessary, attack or even kill. The male brain is not primed for the same access to emotions and the language to express it. We are neurologically different.

That's why, depending on a man's 'wiring' and the quality of his relationship with his inner feminine, it can take him two to three days to come back to a woman to discuss something they passionately shared about in relation to her feelings. He has to travel over the corpus callosum (which sits between the right and left hemispheres) to the other side of his brain to feel the emotion and then find the corresponding language before he can travel back over the brain's Himalayas (corpus callosum) to plant his flag and express it to his woman.

Primary Feminine Principles:
1. Yielding.
2. Receptivity: The willingness and readiness to receive.
3. Vulnerability: the willingness to be truly seen as we are in each given moment.
4. Transparency: the willingness to be completely honest and free of personal agenda.

Primary Masculine Principles:
1. Focus: concentrated and constant effort to achieve an outcome.
2. Freedom: without constraint - to repeatedly release into nothingness.

If a man is predominantly masculine at his core, then he'll have specific predilections and motivations based on what he thinks and does. He'll process information and input through different sensory pathways and neurology than a feminine woman.

If a woman is essentially feminine, then she'll intuit the optimal way. She feels into situations - using her innate energetic and emotional intelligence and then moves out into her day from there. She likes to talk, collaborate and share.

The state of our internal yin and yang is reflected back to us from outside. An awareness of whether our yin or yang is in the driver's seat changes the way we live, attract and manifest, create, relate, process and execute our tasks.

We back ourselves when we create an honest and respectful relationship between these complementary elements.

With embodied practices, we can move between the two at will. A deeper intelligence within us knows when to use our masculine or feminine instead of it using us.

For women, they can shift out of yang mode into their feminine receptivity for better health, sex, and intimacy, creativity and abundance.

Men and Women In their divine union or wholeness of Yin and Yang have better relationships, greater overall productivity, better internal chats with themselves when the going gets tough, more authentic intimacy and mind-bogglingly better sex.

Right orientation of our yin and yang deepens our communion with something far greater than ourselves.

Women Shifting Back into Receptivity
women living life solely from masculine aspects of our nature like intellect and problem solving, tuning into our feminine intuition can be challenging.

A woman battling in her business life with Xena-like ferocity, drawing from her inner masculine drive, may accomplish her outer world goals – but at what cost to her inner world? And at what costs to her relationships?

For a heterosexual woman, If she then goes home to her masculine partner/ husband or lover wielding her axes with both hands there is no diagonally oppositional balance between the couple.

Both are polarised in the masculine.
The relationship becomes based on competitive friendship rather than a healthy delicious charge between the feminine and masculine essence. Resentment inevitably builds when neither party gets their core needs met. Their deepest longing remains unfulfilled.

Men support women more often when they feel them embodied in their feminine energy. They may not be able to quite put their finger on it, but they feel it! It's a primal thing.

They no longer see us as competition but as an empowered woman that deserves to be lifted.

Appendix 5

Menopause Mastery
by Moira Williams

Hormones are powerful! They actually represent Life and Death. They motivate our desire to procreate for the purpose of populating the Earth, and their eventual depletion from our body gradually prepares us for leaving the Earth and returning Home. In between they can heighten the emotional reactions to life.

Even before we begin to experience their power throughout puberty, the menstrual cycle and menopause, we witness the power of the Emotional body through the cycles of the Moon.

These cycles reveal emotional outbursts in children and the desire to be heard in the winter (mature) years. This may be expressed as wisdom gained throughout life or a last ditch effort to release unexpressed emotions. All in all the human body seems to be fuelled by emotions which are governed by hormones. Balance is needed!!

When reflecting back on my own life during these winter years, it is much easier to see that the issues highlighted throughout all of these powerful cycles were a gift to understanding the purpose of the individual's journey on this Earth.

The monthly cycle can be powerful in illuminating the imbalance of the male and female energies within ourselves, which is then reflected in our personal relationships. The male aspect in us all is the doing (Yang energy) and the female is the receiving (Yin energy). Another way to look at it is seeing the male as the Mind (thinking, planning, taking action) and the female as the heart (feeling, receiving, nurturing).Throughout the monthly cycle, the male and female aspect is magnified to assist in observing what is out of balance, so that the Mind and Heart can find solutions and bring Life back into balance. This is often dismissed as premenstrual tension.

Men go through this emotionally too, but have been trained from a very young age to dismiss their feelings and deep inner knowing as weakness and vulnerability. As an Emotional and Spiritual Healer, I have witnessed the need for men to release these rigid beliefs and access a deeper aspect to themselves. They may not have the clarity of an obvious monthly cycle, but they too need to understand their own deep inner wiring and spiritual purpose, and women can assist them with this knowledge.

There are energetic tools such as Astrology and Numerology to explain the internal 'electrical' wiring of each individual. Once understood, it is much easier to identify the emotional and mental reaction to this internal wiring when the hormones increase the intensity.

There is a purpose that women are encouraged to recognise through their menstrual cycle...they are the nurturers (the Yin energy) and they need to teach the wisdom of nurturing by living the Truth and nurturing themselves.

The menstrual cycle highlights and illuminates the need for personal nurturing. If women can take the time to go within and allow the cycle to guide them with the support of their loved ones, they can gradually create balance and peace within themselves, which will then flow into their personal environment. By example, they are showing others how to do the same. The reward for this... menopause can be a much more graceful transition into being the Wise And Unconditionally Loving Woman the Earth needs.

As issues are expressed with clarity throughout each month, it becomes illuminating for all involved, and a loving, supportive environment can be maintained. This takes practice and is the path of the Teacher and Leader, to live the Truth and create a foundation for others to know how to find the same within themselves. By slowing down, going within, listening to inner wisdom, letting go of reactive emotions, communicating and then opening to receiving love and support, it is possible to create more love and peace on the Earth, beginning from within each and every human being....with women leading the way through their monthly cycle.

My own personal journey has been an incredible and valuable learning experience to this process. My experience of premenstrual tension revealed itself each month as a need to do more, have things perfect, play the role that everyone needed me to be without a need to receive nurturing or live peace and tranquillity.

In hindsight, this played out in my childhood beautifully, and when i learnt more about myself through Astrology and Numerology, I saw how my cycle was actually reflecting these same issues . It soon became my best friend and teacher when I listened and trusted my inner knowing.

I was blessed to have a taste of the result in my late forties.....to have the feeling of Heaven on Earth and Mastering the Emotions. My cycle no longer held the triggers it once did. I had ticked everything I needed to address at this point of my life according to some amazing Spiritual mentors I knew.

They explained I hadn't quite finished off the emotional body, the emotional issues to do with victim consciousness and persecution, and as I healed this I would see it reflected in Society. They explained it was deep cellular healing from past lives and family generational healing. Yes, that was true; there had been much domestic violence in my family history. Even though that wasn't my personal experience, it had still definitely been one of control and a lack of nurturing.

And you guessed it, Menopause was the time to reveal the emotional issues I still had left to deal with.

I could have blamed menopause for what was happening but I

understood it was magnifying the need to receive and be nurtured (my monthly cycle). I made the necessary changes in my life to meet this need and I was soon back to living the ebb and flow of peace and loving support.

As I progressed through menopause in my early fifties I found many ways to nurture myself and continued to enjoy the benefit of the hormones my body produced until my early sixties.

Emotionally, mentally and spiritually I felt in balance but physically my body was now beginning to show signs of its own struggle.

As part of my nurturing routine I have always had a six monthly blood test, and it was evident my Oestrogen was negligible. I chose to replace my hormones under the guidance of medical and alternative professionals, and continued to have the regular blood tests, which reaffirmed that my need to use these hormones was minimal to maintain the balance. This, of course, is an individual decision, as is any remedy to obtain homeostasis in the physical body.

My lifestyle at sixty-`four continues to be a reflection of my emotional well being and a willingness to observe the cycles of the moon, meditate, communicate and nurture my own body as I live peace, balance and have a zest for an active life.

The Universe loves and supports us all on our Life's journey and by working through the monthly journey of hormonal changes it becomes evident we have the Power to Create Love, Peace and Balance.

Wishing you much Love, Peace and Balance Always
Moira xx

Appendix 6

Nurture Through The Cycles

A Man's Guide - Navigating the menstrual mood swing is a beautiful and timely call to the healing of the Sacred Wound. We are in the midst of an extraordinary era of Awakening and the most transformational healing that is underway is the balancing of the Sacred Feminine and the Sacred Masculine. Our gendered relationships have been the site of much trauma through the eons and for many people there is a wounding still needing to be healed.

I was not ever a woman who suffered through my cycles and was sometimes suspicious of women who did. In a world in which women are structurally disadvantaged in their access to power, PMT and bleeding are a lever of relief and respite that can be pulled with some confidence that the need for retreat will be respected. To be fair, I wasn't really in touch with my body either and it took me decades to find my way home.

Now in my early fifties, and despite everything I have been taught about menopause and post menopause, I am having the best time of my life on every level. My sex life is extraordinary and all about quality over quantity (think a five star degustation meal compared to a mid-range restaurant!), my energy levels are the best they have ever been, I am at last at home in my face and body and my creative output is a delightfully expanding area of my life. I feel rejuvenated and empowered. Had I believed the stories of post menopause – thickening waste line, dead or dying libido, thinning hair, depression, increased ageing, I would be living in a very different reality. I am in the radiant Autumn of my life, my own poetry in motion.

These days my community and tribe are filled with young women empowering themselves in their bodies and honouring the sacredness and Magick* of their blood. I am excited for the world we are co-creating:

more Red Tents; Blood Moon Dance parties; celebrations and rites of passage for women as they begin to bleed and as their bleeding ends. I feel so fortunate to be embracing the Autumnal flush of my life, to feel my true beauty and sensuality coming alive and to know women in their Spring and Summer and Winter becoming similarly empowered. A glorious New World is dawning, one in which we will all be equal and free.

I love that Meg has written this book for men. Like the Earth, the bodies and rhythms of the women in your life are influencing your own bio-rhythms. We have coherent science to explain that, what once we thought was matter, is actually energy, and the language of energy is frequency. We stand on the outer rim of an ancient magnetic pull that is as old as time itself. Tuning into the frequencies of the cycles of the women in your life will help you tune into your own frequencies which in turn will help you tune into the Earth. We all long to feel more connected to each other and to Mother Earth. Your embodied experience of these frequencies is a fast track path to a greater sense of connection with All That Is.

If you are a woman reading this book and your cycles are giving you suffering and pain, know that your body has unlimited potential to heal and grow strong and to enjoy the seasons of its fertility. The light-hearted nature of Meg's voice in this book is the key here. It's time for us to revel in the extraordinary experience of being embodied as Woman! And yes, Her body is mapped with stretch marks and track marks and tumours and wounds and maybe some days your body feels like this too. But you have chosen to be here as a woman at this time so you could have a direct line of connection to Her rhythmic pull. Rise up and feel your power!

What I love most about Meg's book is there is a far deeper conversation layered and textured through the narrative. Metaphorically speaking, the Sacred Wound in our gendered relations reflects the wounding in our relationship to the Earth, our Mother. We have subjugated and enslaved Her abundance and fertility for our own purposes and now Her cycles are off kilter and the climate is weirding. What we need is for Her natural cycles to re-establish themselves. Sounds impossible, right? What could we possibly do to help make this happen?

All over the world people are using quantum science to manifest miracle healings in their bodies. Near death experience stories from around the world have consistent themes of unconditional Love on the other side of the veil. The marriage of the language of science and the faith of mysticism perhaps gives us the tools to manifest a miracle healing for the Earth. Are we brave enough to try?

To pull off a healing of such a grand scale we need to change the way we understand ourselves and each other. In the grand scope of the cosmic weave of Creation we have lived its paradigms completely. On this extraordinary human journey we have travelled, we have had the opportunity to fully explore its duality. You have been both perpetrator and victim, you are both masculine and feminine. There is no-one to blame, no-one to forgive. *We have co-created every single moment of our journey and we did this with good reason.* In our deepest darkest wounds is the alchemy of our greatest healing. There is no wound so deep as the Sacred Wound between us as men and women.

Meg's book is full of the keys to our transcendence. Through compassion and deep listening to your body and tuning in gently to the rhythms and cycles of all the beautiful people in your life, you will start to resonate a frequency of healing. It's about getting more Yin in your Yang and more Yang in your Yin, right? It's about us getting a bit more groove and swing in our gendered dance. It's about play and gentleness and self-responsibility. It's about tuning my frequencies to your frequencies. It's about "there is a planet to heal - yeah baby this is how we roll!" This is co-created quantum healing at its finest and the best news is it's fun!

To be human is to resist change until the pain of staying where we are is greater than the pain of changing. We all want to feel at home and safe in our bodies. We all want a peaceful healthy planet, but as long as we live in a state of separation from each other and from Her, this is impossible. In this Sacred Ecosystem of Us, you have one responsibility, and this is to heal. The healing of the Sacred Wound is Sacred Work. Embrace it with gentle, Sacred Intent and watch the world begin to heal around you.

A Man's guide is a wise, warm, witty and whimsical reminder that as we come together as brothers and sisters honouring each other as children of the Earth, we will be co-creating the frequencies of healing on a global scale. Bring it!

Deborah is an archetypal and frequency healer, intuitive and holistic counsellor, Kambo and EFT practitioner, Earth lover, community builder, gut health and nutrition nerd and on an extraordinary journey of becoming herself. Find her at www.theactivatedself.com.au

Magick spelled thus is any action that moves us towards our Divine Destiny. It is the expression of True Will and like all energy, it exists as a frequency. It may or may not have any connection to the conscious practice of Magick.

Appendix 7

An Undefended Heart
by Filippa Araki (compassionlounge.com)

Do you long for deeper and more meaningful connections in your life? Do you yearn to feel more appreciated and cherished?

What does it take for us to really open our hearts and start loving each other wholeheartedly? I believe that we all just want to love and be loved, to cherish and be cherished, to desire and be desired.

What is it that makes us have such defended hearts? What is it that holds us back from really showing and expressing how much we love each other? I think it's fear.

Fear that we're going to be rejected.
Fear that we'll lose ourselves in the other person.
Fear that our love won't be reciprocated.
Fear that we'll lose our freedom.

It's so much easier to criticise than to praise, to see each other's faults more than our strengths. And this leads to further and further detachment.

I struggled with these issues in my 27-year marriage. My husband died of cancer earlier this year. He had never been a particularly affectionate or demonstrative person. This was partly cultural, as he was Japanese, partly the tough experiences he'd had as a child, and other factors. In contrast, I am a very tactile person who loves physical affection and words of love. It was challenging for us to find the balance with each other and we had the classic dance of so many relationships — one wanting more and one wanting less.

He said I was demanding. I said he was detached. Finally, I learnt to surrender and let go and just to love and accept him as he was. He then started to relax. About six years ago, he told me that he felt free for the first time in our relationship. Things improved between us, but I still wanted more — more love, more cherishing, more intimacy, more affection. We were also stuck in the modern struggles of financial stress, both working full-time, work schedules that didn't match, raising kids and so on. So hard to find time to just be together and focus on our relationship!

In his year of struggling with his terminal cancer, he went into survival mode and detached further. As his carer, I also became detached. He was convinced he would live. I knew he was going to die, and I was angry that he wasn't savouring every damn last minute with me and the children. Finally, in the last ten days before he died, I got through to him by telling him that if he died, he wasn't going to lose us, that we were going to lose him, because we would still be in the physical body, in the human experience, mostly experiencing each other with our five senses. I begged him to write something for each of us so that we would have some recent words of his to comfort ourselves with. He agreed.

Now, whenever I walked into his room, he poured love and gratitude into me. He told me how much he had always loved me, that he could only have been with me. He told me what a wonderful mother I am and how happy he was to have kids with me. It was a relief, but it was also very painful. Why wait until the end of our lives together to tell each other how much we mean to each other?

My plea to you is — love your loved ones up every day or as often as possible. What I know now is that I gave up too easily early on in our relationship. I believed him, that I was too demanding, too much. My regret is that I didn't strive harder to find the ways around our defenses. I know that we were both doing the best we could with what we had, but I also know that I won't give up so easily again. I have learnt that the way to love is with an undefended heart.

So, how can you cultivate an undefended heart? Focus on what you love about your partner, your children, your family and friends, and tell them. Tell them often. Ask for what you want in positive terms and not through criticism. Express your feelings, both positive and negative. Tell them how you feel, not what you think. Don't get hung up on the story. What is it that really matters to you? Is it really about the dishes? Or is it that you want to know that you matter to them? Be honest. Don't pretend. Don't perform. Be vulnerable. Be yourself. Show the way by dropping your armour first. Undefend your heart and others' hearts will follow suit.

Filippa Araki is passionate about sharing the tools and insights of Compassionate Communication (NVC) that have transformed her inner and outer life. Through decades of personal questing and growth, Filippa gained personal experience of the radical difference that conscious communication skills make in relating to self, others and the environment. By developing an inner space of self-compassion and understanding, we bring more love, acceptance, and integrity to all our relationships. Mother of two, educator for over 30 years, and an internationally certified trainer in Nonviolent Communication (cnvc.org), Filippa supports others' journeys towards living more lightly on the Earth in connected and sustainable communities.

Learn more about Filippa and her work at **compassionlounge.com**

Where To Now?

Remember to add what feels right to your tool kit and ask us for help when you need it, we have heaps of resources and are always collecting more along the way.

@ meghankurtsauthor@gmail.com

If you would like to know more about A Woman's Guide - The art of the unwind, Meghan has a free 5-page sneak peek of her up and coming book at evohe.com.au.

EVOHE also has a great Self Care page where you can take the Adrenal Fatigue test and follow it up with a Self Care action plan. You will find heaps of other great resources here too.

Meghan also invites you to share in the conversation in both of her private facebook groups.

f Nurture through the Cycles - for women

f A Man's Guide Connect - for men

⊙ And, you are always welcome to connect with us via Instagram Meghan Kurts_Author.

www.ingramcontent.com/pod-product-compliance
Lightning Source LLC
Chambersburg PA
CBHW062111290426
44110CB00023B/2778